Also by Pamela Kristan

The Spirit of Getting Organized:
12 Skills To Find Meaning & Power In Your Stuff

AWAKENING
IN TIME

Practical Time Management
For Those on a Spiritual Path

PAMELA KRISTAN

First published by Dog Ear Publishing
4010 W. 86th Street, Ste H
Indianapolis, IN 46268
www.dogearpublishing.net

ISBN: 978-160844-399-4

Printed in the United States of America

ACKNOWLEDGEMENTS

Those who have participated in my consultations and seminars over the past twenty years have been priceless in showing me the depth and breadth of the time management issue. Because of them I developed the practical techniques you find here. My thanks goes out to them, first and foremost.

Many thinkers have had a profound influence on me as I shaped the concepts in this book. Among them are Jacob Needleman (*Time and the Soul, Money and the Meaning of Life*), Martha Beck (*Steering By Starlight*), Kurt Leland (*Menus for Impulsive Living* and the Charles material), Eckhart Tolle (*The New Earth* Oprah Winfrey Webcast), David Abram (*The Spell of the Sensuous*), Joanna Macy (*World As Lover, World As Self*), and Parker Palmer (*Let Your Life Speak*). Thanks to these people and the many others through whose work I evolved.

I thank those who contributed their wise counsel and professional expertise—Martha Cohen who read the book at every stage over the past few years during our regular meetings; Ronnie DiComo who helped with design and research; Kim Elliott, my more-than copy editor, who made this book the best it could be; Jim Guinness and Dale Rosenkrantz who lent their exquisitely careful eyes to the work at the very end; and the many others who read parts of the book as it grew.

Thanks to my buddies who give me strength and support—Susan Douglass, Jim Guinness, Ronnie DiComo, my roommate Brad

Brockmann, my long-time therapist Mark Weber who witnessed so much change over the years, and Monica Dimino my astrologer who spurred me to get this book into your hands in record time. I also thank the people and places of Jamaica Plain, a village within the city of Boston that's ever quirky, restorative, and inviting.

Thanks to you all.

CONTENTS

Acknowledgements v

Part I: Introducing a New Way

Chapter 1: Awakening in the Midst of American Life 3

More + faster ≠ better—the new time management
Look beneath the surface
How the book is set up—Ready, steady, go!

Chapter 2: The Context 7

A brief history of time management (apologies to Stephen Hawking)—
    Escalating pace—Information overload—Homogeneity (same-
    old/same-old)
It's impossible—The remedy
Sustainability—Full cost accounting—Limited resources—To life!
    —A new way

Part II: Attention, Boundaries, Choices

Chapter 3: Awareness, Action, and the ABCs 15

Start from where you are
The ABCs—Attention, Boundaries, Choices

Chapter 4: Attention—Focused and Flexible 17

Presence—Making the change
Attention practice—The pause button—CDR-catch, distribute,
    review—The tickler file—Attention "range of motion": pre-
    sent/future/past, negative/positive, immersion/surface, aligning
    body/mind/heart/spirit

Habits of mind—Expectations, and then—Reality check—Loosening the patterns—Learning from the patterns—Satisfaction—Is satisfaction selfish?

The heartbeat challenge—Both/and not either/or—From "my heartbeat" to "my agenda"—Entrainment

Start from where you are, again

Chapter 5: Boundaries—Protected and Connected 35

Boundaries mediate between inside and outside—Core and periphery

Task boundaries—molding events from the river of experience—Three-phase close-down: the past, the future, the present—How closing down helps: procrastination, lack of focus, doing it until it's done, doing what fits into the time available, neglecting what we need to do for what we want to do, feeling overwhelmed—Variations on a theme: continuing after a close-down, start-up as well as close-down, Mozart and multi-tasking

Transitions

Personal boundaries—Replenishing resources: physical, emotional, mental, spiritual—Boundary challenges: feelings point to the middle way, expand or contract, on my square

A conduit for the energy of life

Chapter 6: Choices—In Tune with Self and Others 53

Conscious or not?—From flat to perspective—Start here and ripple out

Choose what feels good—The cascade of implications—Negative navigation—Feel good practice—More on feelings—Choosing shows us who we are

Challenges to choosing—Untangling the factors: quick and easy, the untangling game—Wanting to do it right: loosening our grip on what's "right"—Having to say "No" in order to say "Yes"

Both/and balance—A technique for achieving balance

The greater good of all—The holon

Part III: Change, and What It Brings

Chapter 7: Change 73

*The path—ever steady progress to the shining goal or ... —
Punk eke—Progress and integration—What to do while waiting
for change to show up*

*Turning bad stuff into good stuff—Internal allies: Curious Anthropol-
ogist, Bold Explorer, Creative Artist, Compassionate Witness—
Truth-telling—Scouting for feeling-habits—The leverage
point—Applying effort: raising awareness; rewriting the script;
taking action; desire, willpower, and guilt—Three feeling-habits:
irritated, anxious, discouraged—The results—acceptance, tolerance
for good feelings, kindness to ourselves*

Helpful techniques: gaining traction, the reset button, external allies

Change is what life is all about

Chapter 8: The Fruits of the Practice 89

*Vitality—Feeling alive only when... —Feeling alive, period—The
way in life*

*Creativity—Expression—Integritas, consonantia, claritas—A musical
example*

*Discernment—Letting go—Hozho, the tightrope walker, and
Goldilocks*

Personal evolution: satisfaction, sovereignty, service—A grand project

*The greater evolution—Nature backs you up, and vice versa—Laying
down tracks*

Part IV: Resources

Further reading...103

Useful practices 105

Feeling-habits..121

PART I

INTRODUCING
A NEW WAY

CHAPTER 1

AWAKENING IN THE MIDST OF AMERICAN LIFE

So many of us are on a spiritual path. We're cultivating presence through various spiritual practices. We're acknowledging our interconnectedness and taking our places in the web of life. We're assuming responsibility for the choices we make and the realities we create. We're dropping old patterns of behavior.

This awakening is happening in the midst of modern America where intense time pressure permeates the atmosphere. The speedy electronic devices that mediate so much of our experience leave us feeling wired, overwhelmed, and forever behind. Awash in a tidal wave of information, we're aware of everything we could (or should) do and our expectations rise with the flood.

There's no time for planning. Projects take longer than we expect. We start things but never finish them. Priorities are out of whack. People constantly interrupt us. We struggle to keep everybody happy. We're always putting out fires. How can we stem the tide and live an authentic spiritual life in such an environment?

More + Faster ≠ Better

We try staying later, working more, or moving faster. Even so, we suspect that won't solve the problem. If we want to survive (and even thrive) in this environment, we know we've got to embrace something else than More + Faster = Better. It's not quantity we seek, but quality—richness, satisfaction, simplicity, complexity, juiciness. And for that we need to break pace, step back, and change.

The New Time Management

There are plenty of magazine articles, TV shows, workshops, and books to tell us how to change. These tips, however, work much like conventional medicine's symptom-oriented prescriptions. Interrupted? Just close your door. Procrastinating? Just break it down. Trouble deciding? Just prioritize. We end up with layers of tips as thick as our To Do lists!

So, what shall we do instead? A close look at the definition of the term "management" helps. The word, manage, comes from the Latin, manus, meaning hand. Managing is, intrinsically, hands-on. The Oxford English Dictionary goes on to say, "to manage is to control the course of affairs by one's actions; to take charge; to use carefully; to operate on for a purpose; to cope with the difficulties of."[1] This is what the new time management is all about: taking charge, carefully, consciously, purposefully—not shrinking from difficulties, but engaging them.

It can be daunting to take charge in a More + Faster = Better atmosphere, but this is exactly what we must do to sustain ourselves, our relationships, and life on the planet. If we manage with respect for ourselves and all beings, "better" takes on a new meaning—contributing to our own evolution and that of the world.

Look Beneath the Surface

In this book, we dig down to the root of the troubles rather than trying to fix the myriad symptoms that crop up like stones in a New England pasture. Beneath most time management troubles are issues of Attention, Boundaries, and Choices—the ABCs of the new time management. For instance, getting distracted is an issue of Attention. When we learn how to maintain internal focus while responding to what's happening around us, the issue resolves. Feeling torn between several demands is a matter of Boundaries. When our boundaries are appropriately firm yet flexible, we can consider demands from both the outside and the inside. Having too much to do in too little time is an issue of Choice. When we learn how to choose what serves the greater good, we can let go of the rest.

Working at this level, change has a better chance of taking hold and many of the surface problems resolve themselves. The practice of managing time infuses our lives with spirit, moment by moment, attending to the inward and the outward, the wide perspective and the everyday details of life. We shift from doing more and doing it faster to engaging fully and appropriately with life.

This book does not espouse a particular spiritual path since many people today draw on various teachings and experiences built up over the years for their spirituality. Truth no longer has a capital T— it's evolving as we evolve. The tools and insights presented here are in tune with this eclectic view of spirituality.

How the Book Is Set Up

Here you will find a mix of practical, hands-on techniques and new ways of thinking. You'll learn how to become more present. You'll experiment with working cheerfully within the limits of time, space, and the body. You'll become more vital, more fully who you are meant to be. You'll cultivate a sense of deep satisfaction despite the impossibility of doing it all.

You'll start by taking a look at the context—reflecting on the particular challenges we all face today and how principles of sustainability can help us meet these challenges.

Next, you'll encounter the ABCs—Attention, Boundaries, and Choices—exploring new ways of thinking and acting in each area.

After you work with the ABCs, you'll turn to the change process itself. You'll learn how challenges, mistakes, and difficulties can help us as much as our accomplishments and triumphs. Everything we do, "good" or "bad," can move us along.

Lastly, you'll reap the fruits. You'll see how the new time management promotes the capacities of vitality, creativity, and discernment, and contributes to the greater good of all.

The practices explained in the text (plus many more) appear in Part IV—the Resource section. This section also expands on some concepts that the text just touches upon.

Throughout the book, concepts reappear in different guises so you see them from many points-of-view. Each encounter may touch you at a different level. Each may resonate for you in a different way. Feel free to skip around rather than read straight through. This is a book to pick up and put down, to read a little bit and then let it sink in. Use it in a way that makes sense to you.

Ready, Steady, Go!

You're about to embark on a journey that could change your life. You won't be alone—many bold explorers have gone before you. You'll have help—the practices in this book are reliable supports. You'll spark your creativity as you respond to familiar situations in new ways. You'll learn about yourself and practice compassion as you walk this perilous, demanding, revealing, and ultimately satisfying path. Do come along!

CHAPTER 2

THE CONTEXT

To appreciate today's time management challenges we need to grasp the context in which these challenges arise. As it turns out, nothing like what we face has ever happened before in the history of our world—ever. To get a sense of what we face today, we've got to go back—to the beginning.

A Brief History of Time Management (Apologies to Stephen Hawking)

In "the beginning," as many of our stories say, the earth was without form. Back then there was no time management, since there was effectively no time. (Or you could say there was all the time in the world!) The Creator's first act in Western religion's tales was to "let there be light," separate it from darkness, and make day and night.

Once humans came on the scene they found there were things they could do during the day that they couldn't do at night. No doubt, they very quickly found themselves making choices about what to do when. And what is this, but … time management! So, folks arranged their lives in tune with the natural cycles of the sun, the moon, and the seasons.

The Greek myth of Prometheus, the fire-bringer, points us in the direction of the situation in which we find ourselves today. With Prometheus's gift, people could gather around the fire and do all kinds of things they hadn't been able to do at night. It was a great technological development but, like all good things, there was another side to it. Those who used fire had to make sure it didn't get out of control.

Since Prometheus, there has been a long line of technological inventions that have loosened the hold that the "givens" of life have on us. The one that has happened in our lifetime might well have as great an impact on time management as Prometheus's fire. We all know what it is—The Electronic Revolution, with its proliferation of computers and other devices, both in the workplace and at home.

Forget about the givens of time and space! Now we can communicate instantaneously. We have access to formerly unimaginable amounts of information. We can work or play any time, any place. All well and good, as long as we acknowledge that the benefits of the electronic age have come at a price.

Escalating Pace

Consider how turn-around expectations have changed. Before computers, it took at least a week for a business communication to come full circle—several days to dictate, draft, edit, produce, and post a letter; several days for it to arrive; and several days to dictate, draft, edit, produce, and post a reply. Nowadays, if you haven't responded to a nine o'clock e-mail by ten, you get a call wanting to know what's up. Talk about a change in response expectations—from one week to one hour!

Electronics have had a subtle impact on how we expect life to proceed, moment-to-moment. When we say, "I'll be there in a minute," it's as if we were a mouse click away. We leave in a rush, resent the red light on our way, and arrive breathless and irritated fifteen minutes later. Think of it—we resent a red light!

Our speedy machines have engendered a false sense that there's no limit to how fast we can go. Although we can't hit our personal "Send" button to arrive at our destination instantaneously, deep down, we expect to do so. There's an undercurrent of frustration, resentment, and shame about the conditions of life on Earth, about our needs for sleep, society, love, exercise, and everything else that humans need and computers don't.

Information Overload

We can access a dizzying amount of information. In *Information Anxiety*, Richard Wurman says that the amount of information in a single daily *New York Times* is equivalent to that encountered by a seventeenth century literate person in an entire lifetime.[2] And this is just print information. Think about what comes via TV and the Internet. Do we really think that in the few hundred years since the century of Shakespeare and Descartes we've increased our capacity to assimilate information all that much? Doubtful.

We're aware of what's happening on the other side of the globe; what possible vacations we could take; how we should be parenting, taking care of our bodies, or performing at work. Having this information ramps up our expectations to in fact do something about the situation on the other side of the globe, or have a stupendous vacation, or be a great parent. In his book *The Paradox of Choice*, Barry Schwartz states that knowing about these possibilities doesn't make it any easier to choose among them.[3]

Homogeneity (Same-Old / Same-Old)

Since work can happen any time, any place, one day becomes like the next. No longer are there special times when the stores close and families gather around the table. When we go on vacation, we stay "plugged in" by constantly checking our e-mail and voice mail. For many of us, 24/7/365 is relentless—one moment is just like the last, and the next, and the next. It's no surprise that our culture ramps up the intensity to counter this homogeneity. It seems that the volume in movies is louder, street lights are brighter, food is spicier, and the media are more violent. Then, when there's "nothing to do," we're impatient, bored, and uncomfortable with "peace and quiet."

It's Impossible

As technology's pace escalated, we assumed we could keep up by staying a bit later, working at home, or coming in on the weekend.

Each escalation has come gradually, so we've become habituated to the changes as they've come. However, if we could jump from twenty years ago to today, we would see the situation as it is and say, unequivocally, "This is impossible."

The fact is—it IS impossible. We can't do it all. No one can. We can't read every book, magazine, or paper we hear about. We can't buy everything we see on TV or the Internet. We can't take advantage of all the opportunities we encounter, even if they're wonderful, healthful, and life-affirming. It's just plain impossible—impossible to do everything everyone else wants us to do, and even impossible to do everything we think we really need to do. For some, this is disappointing news ("You mean I *can't* do it all?"); for others, it's liberating ("You mean I *don't have to* do it all?").

And, in fact, we're not doing it all. Very few people actually do everything on their lists (I certainly don't!). We do some things and not others. We make choices all the time. The challenge is to acknowledge that we're not doing it all anyway, and then make those choices more consciously.

The Remedy

We're in a perfect situation to do things differently. More and more people are realizing that the way they're living isn't sustainable. They work too much, don't get enough sleep, jeopardize their health, and compromise their relationships, their civic life, and their spirituality. The remedy is not to speed up or even, really, do more. There will always be more to do, and the machines will always be faster. Rather, we would be wise to develop our internal authority, instead of using machines as our measure or automatically accepting external norms.

The new time management gives us the skills we need to make these changes. It takes our humanity, in its entire earthiness, into account. It protects us from the onslaught of information, demands, and expectations. It sharpens our discernment so we base our choices on what's good for ourselves and our world.

Sustainability

The principles of sustainability apply to time as well as any other resource. With the new time management, we take into account all the costs and benefits of how we use time, not just the obvious ones. We work within the limits of our time and energy. We promote general well-being by living in harmony with natural laws.

Full Cost Accounting

Sustainable systems account for all costs and benefits. On the time management cost side, we acknowledge that staying up late jeopardizes the next day's energy; that the lack of a reminder system breeds anxiety; that doing little, peripheral tasks compromises attention to the important tasks at the core of our lives.

On the benefit side, we acknowledge that taking real breaks generates energy; that we can find deep satisfaction in a job imperfectly done; that taking time to cultivate friendship sustains life beyond the job. Our culture often undervalues—or doesn't even recognize—these benefits (similar to not accounting for "women's work" in the Gross National Product). Taking all the costs and benefits into account gives us a more realistic picture. From this wider, more comprehensive perspective, our time management choices make sense.

Limited Resources

Sustainable systems acknowledge that resources have limits. Nowhere is this more obvious than with time. Regardless of how powerful, rich, or technologically advanced we may be, or how worthy, entitled, or needy we might be, we still get twenty-four hours in a day and that's it. Period. There is no more time.

Consider the bleary-eyed student handing in the paper she wrote all last night saying, "It would've been better if I'd had more time," to which the professor replies, "Well, you had all the time there is!" It's true. We have all the time in the world, right now, and always. So it's not a question of getting more, but of using what we have well.

There's also a limit to our energy, but in this case, we can actually generate more. We can replenish our energy resources as we go. Rather than charging forth, full-steam ahead, we can monitor our energy and respond to our needs for rest and rejuvenation (and not pump ourselves up with stimulants). In the end, this way of operating is sustainable; the other way leads to burnout.

To Life!

Sustainable systems enhance life; they make things better in the long run—not by having more options or features, but by being more satisfying and contributing to the greater good. Sustainable systems operate in tune with natural law. In the new time management we extend ourselves, and we relax, just as organisms rest at times and are active at other times. We say "Yes" to some things and "No" to others, just as the cell membrane allows some substances in and keeps others out. When we operate as nature does, nature backs us up and supports us.

A New Way

We are at a crossroads in our development as humans. If we choose to continue as things are now, we're on the road to burnout. However, as sovereign, self-aware beings, we have the capacity to do something different—to take our lives in hand and create for ourselves a new way of being that will carry us into the future.

PART II

ATTENTION,
BOUNDARIES,
CHOICES

CHAPTER 3

AWARENESS, ACTION, AND THE ABCS

Developing new skills depends on awareness and action—seeing what we need to do and doing it. Awareness helps us see problems clearly. We know the history, we see the context, and we acknowledge what's actually happening. Taking action is, of course, doing things differently. Although we resist change mightily, our natural desire to grow helps us along.

Awareness and action feed each other. Sometimes awareness comes first. Say, we notice that some tasks are slipping through the cracks because we have reminders in three different places. Then we take action and set up a central reminder collecting area. Other times, action comes first. We might get a new style of planner and only then realize how cumbersome the old system was.

We need a balance of awareness and action for a well-lived life. Few of us choose the life of a cloistered contemplative where there's a maximum of awareness with a minimum of action. Most of us live in the midst of contemporary life, and our days are full of maximum action with minimal awareness. The American norm of extreme busy-ness makes it difficult to step back and reflect.

In his book, *Money and the Meaning of Life*, Jacob Needleman tells of a fourteenth century religious order, the Brotherhood of the Common Life, in which men and women practiced "the mixed life, uniting action and contemplation in the midst of daily activity."⁴ Such a "way in life," with its balance of awareness and action, operates in the middle ground where life is rich, satisfying, and engaging.

Start From Where You Are

It may be obvious that we can only start from where we are, but that's not what usually happens. Our wish to be something different than what we are disposes us to start from where we would like to be. The trick of starting where we are, of course, is to recognize where that is—and that takes some doing. Kindly, courageous awareness—both compassionate and dispassionate—allows us to be in a truthful, yet humane relationship with ourselves.

Because this relationship with ourselves is so fraught, difficult, and often elusive (like trying to track down a wild animal!), throughout the book you'll learn skills to help yourself first and then widen out to the larger context of family, friends, colleagues, work, community, and world. The skills you learn for yourself apply just as well to these larger circles. In time, you'll find that becoming aware of yourself and taking helpful action on your own behalf benefits all the circles to which you belong.

The ABCs

In the three chapters that follow, you'll use both awareness and action to work below the surface symptoms of time management distress. You'll focus on the deeper level where lasting change, not just symptomatic relief, is possible. The areas of inquiry are Attention, Boundaries, and Choices—the ABCs of sustainable time management.

You'll cultivate focused, yet flexible attention to either hold onto the thread through distractions or let go when it's time to stop. You'll learn how to establish task boundaries that contain what you do and allow you to make graceful transitions between tasks. You'll learn how to set appropriate interpersonal boundaries that protect your uniqueness while connecting you effectively and compassionately to others. You'll learn how to make good time management choices in tune with your truest values and grounded in what's actually possible. The skills you develop will stand you in good stead to meet whatever time management challenges come your way.

CHAPTER 4

ATTENTION—
FOCUSED AND
FLEXIBLE

Managing time depends on our ability to direct our attention.[5] We look over our list, choose a task, and bring our attention there. If, while in the midst of the task, we get interrupted by someone coming in or distracted by our own stray thoughts, we have the presence of mind to stay with our chosen task—or not—as we choose. It seems simple (and in a way, it is), but it's certainly not easy! Entire spiritual systems, both ancient (such as Buddhist meditation) and modern (such as Eckhart Tolle's *The Power of Now*), rest on attention as a core practice.

For most of us, attention is a hit-or-miss kind of affair. Sometimes, we focus on whatever is in front of our noses. Other times, we slide off to the e-mail pop-up, the person walking in, or the ringing phone. Or, maybe we immerse ourselves so deeply in a project that it's hard to come up for air. Each of these modes of attention can be appropriate. Usually, however, we choose a mode out of habit, regardless of whether it is appropriate for a specific task.

When we can consciously direct our attention, we have more options. We can focus on a single point if we need to zero in on details, or we can see the big picture if we need to place a project in context. We can concentrate for a long stretch of time when the task is complex or for a little while if the time available is short. We can reflect on the past to evaluate and assess. We can project to the future to plan and speculate. We can stay in the present to stick to the task at hand.

We develop this attention "range of motion" by softening up habitual patterns and firming up new skills, very much like what we do to develop physical range of motion. This softening and firming process is a lifelong practice. It begins with presence.

Presence

Presence is, simply, conscious contact with ourselves. Presence to ourselves—just showing up[6]—cultivates attention. We notice what's going on, we wake up to our experience, and we become a witness to our own lives. In so doing, we develop a steadier inner core of attention from which to make time management choices.

In our highly stimulating environment, with its never-ending stream of interrupting phone calls, e-mails, and visitors, it's all too easy to let our attention run like a Springer Spaniel on the beach. We talk to the visitor, answer the e-mail, and pick up the phone. Sometimes, we do all three at once!

But, say we want an undistracted half-hour to work on a report. No sooner do we start than our e-mail alert pops up, and we switch from the report to the e-mail. We're so much in the habit of responding that we do it without thinking. There's nothing intrinsically wrong with switching, but our considered intention was to have an uninterrupted half-hour. For that, we need to soften up our automatic response and firm up our capacity to stay with the original task.

This is very much like teaching a dog to "Stay!" when it wants to run off after a squirrel. The dog responds instinctively to the squirrel—it would automatically run off. However, the master has established a learned response with the dog, building on the dog's eagerness to learn and please. The master, having the big picture in mind, sees that it's in everyone's interest for the dog to Stay and not run after the squirrel.

Similarly, in the situation with the report, we can see that in the larger scheme of things it's better to continue with the report than to respond to the e-mail. Even though we want to read the new message, we stay with the report. We see the larger picture and act accordingly. We are aware of our habitual response, *and* we set it aside. (Often we're not even aware that we've slid off until we "wake up" somewhere else; only then do we realize how far off we've gone.)

Making the Change

Awareness is the first step. Next comes Action. Changing a habit is, of course, not so easy. We have grooves in our behavior that we've worn in over time and that we fall into by default. Our surrounding culture—work, family, community, and others—furnishes a full set of grooves as well. Even if we're aware of the groove, it's still a challenge to step out of it. It's uncomfortable, unfamiliar, and awkward.

The attitude to take with ourselves is very much like that of the good dog trainer—both kind and firm. There's no need to beat ourselves up. Every dog slips up. So does every human. We need to be patient with ourselves and, at the same time, hold fast to our intention. We know it's difficult to disengage from habits, yet we take ourselves in hand and give it a try, taking steps that are challenging but not overwhelming.

As we develop the capacity to Stay, we become—like the dog—more reliable, more focused, and able to perform a greater range of "tricks." Most importantly, we become more conscious.

Attention Practice

Developing attention is a lifelong practice rather than something we learn to do once and for all. No one gets it "right" all the time, but it's certainly possible for anyone to get better at it. Designed to exercise your attention "muscles," the following techniques will help you expand your range of behavior and step out of the grooves.

The Pause Button

In this practice, you keep a thread of attention attached to a task in the face of interruptions. It works on the same principle as the Pause button on a movie player. Think of how you use the Pause button. In the middle of the movie, the phone rings. You press Pause to stop the action, take the call, and then press Play to continue.

The practice works for any interruption. Say someone walks in while you're working on a project. At that very moment, you take literally only a few seconds to jot down a word or fix an image in your mind. You might also take a mental "snapshot" of the physical position of your body or the particular pen that's in your hand before you respond to the person. With each of these conscious acts, you press your internal Pause button to stop the action. After you give yourself this time, you respond to the person. When you finish talking to the person, you return to that fixed point and pick up exactly where you left off. These physical, visual, and verbal cues all help fix the Pause point.

In the seminars I lead, I introduce the Pause button at the very beginning so that the participants are ready when the first interruption occurs—someone coming late to a time management seminar! After the newcomer settles in, I turn to the participants and ask, "So, where were we when Joe walked in?" Invariably someone in the room has the exact words spoken at the interruption moment. By the end of the session, all of the participants can use their internal Pause buttons to step out of the flow of events for the two seconds it takes to stop the action, and then step back in at the same spot.

CDR—Catch, Distribute, Review

This technique is particularly helpful when you interrupt yourself. You know how it is—you're working on a report and a thought flits through your mind to pick up the dry cleaning on the way home from work. Your mind then starts shuttling between the report and the dry cleaning, the report and the dry cleaning. If you try to keep the dry cleaning in mind while working on the report, you compromise your attention. Instead, use CDR—Catch, Distribute, Review—to keep your attention where you want it.

First, catch thoughts that run through your mind. There are many ways to do that. You can jot down a trigger note on a sticky, a 3x5 card, a scrap of paper; a steno pad, a little notebook, or a desk calendar. You might leave yourself an e-mail or voice mail. Or, you might choose to put a notation in your computer or PDA.

Although catching ideas is familiar to many of us, it's only the first step of the process. The next step is to distribute the note to where it will make the most sense to review it later. For example, a note for picking up dry cleaning can go in the purse or vest pocket; a note about a specific work project can go in that project's folder.

Many people are just fine at catching ideas, but they let them lie—wherever. This is a perfect set-up for scattered attention (I know I wrote down a note about what to get at the library, but where is it?) If you distribute the notes where you're likely to use them and where similar material resides, it will be much easier to review them.

Keep in mind that "review" does not mean "do." Many people avoid catching the notes or leave them scattered about because they subconsciously think that if they run into that note again they'll have to do it. That's not true. You can still choose whether to do it or not. When the note is with its fellows, it's much easier to make that decision. (The Choices chapter will help with decision-making.)

Here are some CDR tips:

Date each entry—a chronological trigger may help your recall.

Write on only one side of the page so that if you need to physically distribute an entry, you can cut up the page.

Boldly cross out finished items and brightly highlight those still open so it's obvious whether to continue to pay attention to the item or not.

In a funny way, CDR actually has some parallels to CPR. When we try to keep too much in our heads and don't catch our ideas on notes, we can get overwhelmed and paralyzed—sort of like cardiac arrest. When we bounce around, doing whatever comes to mind, we can get caught in frantic, uncoordinated activity—sort of like fibrillation. CDR helps us collect ideas so we can clear our heads, get unstuck, and put our energy where it serves us well.

The Tickler File

The Pause button helps you in the moment. CDR helps you clear your mind for the immediate future. The tickler file helps you manage attention over a longer time frame. It's a method of working with time-sensitive material that allows you to think about something at the appropriate time, but not until then. Say, you have a grant deadline four months down the road. You don't have to work on it now, but you do have to start it in a couple of months. A tickler file can remind you—"tickle you," hence the name—when you need to start in order to meet your deadline.

Ticklers can be paper-based or electronic; the principles are the same. Here's how a paper-based tickler works (see Part IV—the Resource section for more details).

- Make seventeen file folders—one for every month, January through December, and one for every week, 1st, 2nd, 3rd, 4th, 5th.

- Put reminders into appropriate folders, making sure you tickle when you need to start, not end (more on this later).

- At the beginning of the month, distribute the tickles in the month's folder into the week folders (the only month that's broken down into weeks is the current month).

- At the beginning of the week, group what's in that week's folder into days, paper-clip each day's work together, stack the clipped groups with Monday on top and work through the groups, day by day.

- Empty folders go to the back of the system, ready for next year's (or next month's) tickles.

The beauty of the system is that once the tickle is in there, you no longer have to think about it. It will come up when it needs to, so you can keep your mind clear. As you work through the day, move any leftovers or undone reminders to another appropriate day. If a reminder keeps showing up, decide whether to do it or not.

My tickler file resides in the top right file drawer of my desk. The current week's work, the only material not in the tickler, is parked in a vertical sorter on my desk at my right hand. This set-up makes it accessible and easy to use. The virtue of a physical tickler is that you can use the conference brochure, the meeting agenda, or the tax form itself, rather than a separate reminder *about* the conference, meeting, or form. I use 3x5 cards rather than flimsy slips of paper for tickles. For recurring tickles, I re-use the same card. For example, once I've had my car oil changed, I take the same reminder and put it three months hence when I'll need it again.

Remember to tickle where you'll need to start in order to deliver on time. For example, you know you'll need two weeks to finish a report due October 15th, so you put the report reminder in the September folder. For a conference, you tickle the registration deadline, not when the conference occurs. For complex projects, identify major tasks and tickle each segment. Templates for recurring projects may be useful as well.

An electronic tickler works in the same way. Enter reminders in your electronic calendar system, and then access them as the weeks and months progress. Park any supporting paperwork, arranged chronologically, in a handy physical file.

Attention "Range of Motion"

There are many ways to engage attention. Having a wide range of possibilities to call upon gives you flexibility so you can use the mode that's most appropriate to the task at hand. Here are some ways of engaging attention.

Present, future, and past

Being present—Here & Now—is, for the most part, the best place to be when managing time. Yet, there are times when we really need to focus on the future. When we're doing something we've never done before, like putting on a big celebration, we need to project into the future to outline the steps to take. Then, when the celebration is over, we can learn from the past by reflecting on what worked and what didn't. There's a fine line between these helpful orientations and worry about the future or regret for the past. If we keep our awareness non-judgmental, we see that it's all useful information that need not drag us down or make us anxious.

Negative / positive

Generally, focusing on the positive is a helpful orientation. However, there are times when focusing on the negative is exactly what we need to do. For example, when we embark on a risky venture—like a job interview. Anticipating the worst might help us generate useful alternate scenarios. Say, our skills don't match their needs. Even so, we can get networking numbers or ask for advice. Envisioning the worst gives us creative options and builds hardiness so we don't collapse when things don't go as we'd envisioned.

Immersion / surface

We can operate at a level appropriate to the task. We can skim the surface, breezing through lots of relatively simple tasks. Or we can hunker down and immerse ourselves. The danger lies in getting too much in the habit of either level. If all we can do is skim the surface, we lose the richness and complexity that depth offers—we're "spacey" and ungrounded. If all we can do is dive deep, we have trouble switching between tasks—we let other important things fall through the cracks.

Switching between several tasks—multi-tasking—is a mode of attention best suited to surface tasks. You'll explore multi-tasking and how it can work well in the next chapter on task boundaries. Effective multi-tasking depends not only on maintaining a clear core of attention to each task, but also on closing down all the tasks in the "multi-tasking arena."

Aligning body / mind / heart / spirit

When all aspects of ourselves line up, it's easiest to direct our attention. When you notice your attention compromised, check out each of these four aspects of your being. It may be that your body wants some movement, or your heart just isn't in it. If you can bring the aspect on board, that's great. If not, negotiate for some cooperation for a limited time from that aspect.

With a range of tools in your Attention toolbox, you can manage your attention appropriately.

Habits of Mind

These attention practices help us keep our minds appropriately flexible or focused as needed. Why is that so difficult? One reason is that it's not just our minds that are involved, but also our feelings.

Expectations, and Then …

The mind seems to automatically generate a host of expectations based on hopes, fears, past experiences, and judgments. Then, what we expect to happen doesn't actually happen. Here are three scenarios.

> The report we thought we would finish in an hour still isn't ready at the end of the hour.
>
> We're in the middle of writing a friend and our child comes in wanting lunch now.
>
> We find ourselves cranky when just a moment ago we felt fine.

Whatever we had in mind (consciously or subconsciously) isn't what's happening. Instead, it's more difficult, overwhelming, or dull than we'd envisioned. Or it's daunting, uninviting, slow, or boring.

So we get impatient, angry, frustrated, exasperated, indignant, ashamed, disappointed, confused—you name it! All kinds of uncomfortable feelings arise because of this "bait-and-switch."

In the three scenarios, here are possible uncomfortable feelings: We feel frustrated with ourselves for not working fast enough or with others for not getting us the material sooner. We feel hopeless about getting time by ourselves while mothering. We feel guilty about taking a break with the boss breathing down our necks. (Each of us has a familiar repertoire of feelings when things don't go as we expect.)

As long as we view what's happening and our response to it as information, pure and simple, we're OK. But, most often, thoughts and feelings entangle us. We ruminate over similar instances in the past or worry about consequences in the future. We judge ourselves and others, all of which compromises our ability to pay attention to the task at hand.

It's helpful to remember that simple presence to these feelings—acknowledging them, not pushing them away—can help us move through them more easily. Acceptance is the key. This is the way things are at the moment. We can view the discrepancy between our expectations and what is happening as just an observation—information without the spin of judgment. Such a neutral, embracing attitude helps us witness the bumps in the road without trying to eliminate or ignore them, regardless of how unpleasant, uncomfortable, or embarrassing they may be.

Reality Check

The information we gather as we witness these thoughts and feelings can help us manage time. In the examples above, we can acknowledge how long things actually take and base current and future plans on that. We can negotiate with our child for another ten minutes to finish the letter. We can recognize our need for a break and take it. We might even note our feelings (using CDR) so we can process them later.

One client who found herself rushing her child out the door in the morning decided to gather some data. She timed the drive between home and school—first, on a normal day, then on a day with bad weather, and finally on a day when she went as fast and as safely as possible without rushing. She now had a range of real-life times. She did the same thing with the at-home morning routine— how long did it normally take (without rushing!), how long did a leisurely, ultra-comfortable routine take, and how long did the bare minimum take.

It's important to acknowledge how long it takes—not what we hope, or expect, or wish, or imagine it takes, but how long it actually takes. We need to get comfortable with reality as it is, not as our upbringing, the electronic click-environment, the media, or you-name-it, expects it to be. If we go faster than we can, we're creating a set-up for unmet expectations, uncomfortable feelings, and judgments. Better that we gracefully and cheerfully acknowledge the reality of the situation before us.

To do so, it can be helpful to maintain the clear, neutral attitude of the curious anthropologist—keenly interested in everything, yet expecting nothing. That's the challenge—not to let our expectations and the judgments that flow from them compromise presence to what's before us. With this attitude we can stay awake, even in distress, and make better choices. We don't abandon ourselves when the going gets tough.

Loosening the Patterns

Once we start to pay neutral attention, we notice our habits— singing songs in our mind's ear, worrying about what to have for dinner, feeling ashamed about what we said that we shouldn't have said. Most of this mind-chatter has no practical purpose. We've sung that song fifty times already, a perfectly sufficient dinner will be there when we need it, and what we've said is over and done.

This is not to say that mind-singing, planning, and worrying are never of any use, but their usefulness is limited. Singing to ourselves can be enjoyable, planning can help us identify tasks to do, and feeling bad can move us to make amends. Mostly, however, these thoughts and feelings just circle around and around and never go anywhere. There's a wonderful word in German for tunes that keep going through our brains—Ohrwurm, "ear-worm." These thoughts are like a little parasite that insidiously finds its way into our systems and gets stuck there.

Luckily, the mind is trainable. We can clear out some of these marginally useful thoughts and feelings by directing our attention away from them. First, we raise our awareness. Then, when we become aware of the mind dwelling on something we choose not to dwell on, we gently, firmly guide it away. As in training a dog, we need to be both firm and gentle. Enticements and rewards are far more effective than threats and punishments. With a dog, our best ally is the dog's natural desire to please. With ourselves, our best ally is the satisfaction and good feelings we engender when we attend to what we choose.

As we begin to clear out the chatter, we suddenly find we have lots more time! I had a clear demonstration of this when I stopped smoking, a long-term habit that was hard to break. It was only after I quit that I noticed how much time I had spent thinking about smoking—wondering if I had enough cigarettes, planning when I could smoke next, worrying about the time lost taking my smoke break. When cigarettes were no longer a part of my life, I was astonished at how much time, not to mention mental and emotional energy, I had bound up in smoking.

Learning from the Patterns

Patterns can be great teachers. For example, you notice that you habitually think about the future. This is great when starting a new project—you can envision how it might go, outline the steps, and incorporate them into your schedule. But habitual thinking about the future can jeopardize your connection to your present experience. The key is to become aware of the pattern, call on it when appropriate, and not fall into it when it's not appropriate.

For example, you might notice that guilty feelings pop up whenever a friend makes a request you can't honor. You realize that you get flustered when your boss walks in. Or, you find that you resent a colleague who interrupts you in the middle of a writing project. As these patterns grow familiar, you learn more about your particular view of reality. The patterns themselves are neither good nor bad; they're just interesting ways of going about things that sometimes work and sometimes don't. In the section on Change, you'll explore how to find value even in habitual patterns that don't work well.

Satisfaction

A particularly insidious habit of mind is to dwell on dissatisfaction. Our environment is supersaturated with commercial messages that literally bank on our dissatisfaction—with what we have, with what we do, and with who we are—so that we'll buy whatever it is they're selling. No wonder we feel dissatisfied. The media puts before us super-moms, fabulous celebrities, and all kinds of "successful people" who seem to be able to do it all. In comparison to them, we're bound to come up short. Our challenge is to become aware of the pervasive atmosphere of dissatisfaction, consciously disengage from it, and cultivate satisfaction instead.

Awareness is the first step. The attention practices in this chapter can help you establish a steadier core of internal attention that's less at the mercy of every passing message. Stepping back from the flood, you'll begin to see the slant towards dissatisfaction with what's happening here and now. You might try an experiment—experience the messages that come to you—via billboard, radio, print, screen—with a neutral, unengaged objectivity. You'll be astonished at how many of the messages use comparatives (more, better, faster, etc.) that undercut your present experience. You can also practice "not-going-there"—not buying into whatever feelings the commercial media wish would arise in you.

It's easier to disengage from this onslaught of dissatisfaction by having something else to focus on—like satisfaction! This is what I call satisfaction practice. We focus on what we have, rather than what we lack, what we've done rather than what we need to do. We give our accomplishments weight, even if they seem puny at first, for, like a snowball rolling downhill, our accomplishments gather bulk and momentum as we focus on them. We put our attention on what feels good, what serves, what works, what generates joy. Then we begin to feel like we're making progress, like we're getting somewhere.

In our culture, this doesn't come naturally. It takes practice to recognize the fruits of our efforts. But it's a practice that addresses a whole host of time management ills. In the first chapter, you saw that it's literally impossible to do everything. Faced with an endless list of things to do, it's all too easy to get discouraged. There's always more. We're never really done. If the enormity of it all overwhelms us, we can stop dead in our tracks. Yet, satisfaction practice can turn things around. Instead of being overwhelmed and discouraged, we begin to feel energized and encouraged.

Is satisfaction selfish?

There is a delicate distinction between being selfish and serving the greater good through attention to oneself. The classic definition of selfish is fulfilling one's needs at the expense of others' needs. This assumes a separation between self and others—it's an either/or thing. If, however, we maintain a wider focus and keep the greater good of all in mind, our "self-serving" can contribute to fulfilling greater needs.

But can we focus on what feels good, especially when there are people all around the world who feel bad? What right do we have to feel good anyway, unless we've done something heroically painful? In *Finding Your Own North Star*, Martha Beck points out that even though "everybody"—family, peers, the media, religious institutions, organizations—pressures us to deny our satisfaction, our feeling bad really doesn't help other people around the world feel any better.

Physics shows that in actuality, everything is interconnected. How you experience life influences how everyone experiences life. Thus, your satisfaction contributes, in a sense, to the general pool of satisfaction in the world. By enjoying life, you make life more enjoyable. By healing yourself, you heal the world of which you are a part. Think of that! We will explore this concept later on as well.

Systems of thought like The Secret hold that whatever we lend our attention to tends to grow. With that in mind, focusing on what's lacking, what's left to do, what's undone, engenders more lack, more to do, and more things undone. Attending to our accomplishments, to the positive side of things, engenders a greater sense of accomplishment and satisfaction. As we make this fundamental shift, life is no longer so overwhelming, discouraging, and distasteful. Instead, it's fulfilling, encouraging, and delightful.

The Heartbeat Challenge—Both/And Not Either/Or

In my seminars, we do a challenge exercise in each ABC area. The one for Attention involves staying in touch with one's heartbeat. I give people prompts that make it increasingly difficult to stay in touch with their heartbeats. First, they close their eyes and I ask them to find their pulses. Then, I ask them to make sounds in time with their pulses. Next, I ask them to open their eyes while continuing to make their sounds. This is difficult enough, but then I invite everyone to make their sounds considerably louder so that everyone can hear them. The final step is to listen to someone else's sound that's different than theirs while continuing to make their sounds.

Invariably people lose track of their heartbeats somewhere along the way. Some people can't find their heartbeat in the first place. Others are fine until they have to open their eyes. Most lose track of their own sounds when they have to listen to someone else's.

Then we brainstorm what might have made it easier for them to stay with their heartbeats. Some responses have been: using ear plugs to dampen the stimulus, knowing what was going to happen in advance, getting "training" in finding a pulse, or making one's own sound louder.

From "My Heartbeat" to "My Agenda"

What, you might ask, does this have to do with time management? Perhaps, everything! Substitute the words "my agenda" for "my sound" or "my heartbeat" and see what comes up. "I can't even find my agenda in the first place," or "I can stay with my agenda as long as I can be private about it and not have to participate with other people's agendas," or "I get overwhelmed when other people's agendas are strong."

The remedies that help us stay present with our own agendas can work the same way as with the heartbeat sound. "I can put a buffer between myself and the stimulus," "I can get clear on my own agenda beforehand," "I can prepare in advance," or "I can put out my own agenda loud and clear."

This exercise demonstrates a fundamental challenge in time management—to stay in contact with one's own agenda while participating with other agendas. It's a both/and situation, not either/or. Time management works best when we stay connected to our own ideas, plans, and desires in the midst of a complicated matrix of other people's ideas, plans, and desires. You'll explore this concept even further in the next chapter on Boundaries.

Entrainment

During the heartbeat challenge, participants often lock onto a heartbeat rhythm that's close to theirs. This is an example of entrainment. Rhythms that are close to each other tend to get in sync. When that happens, it's actually easier; both people ride the same energy. Think of the "agenda" situation. When someone has an agenda similar to our own, we're together on the issue and it's easier to put ourselves out there.

Entrainment can work with us, and it can work against us. When the rhythms around us aren't anywhere near our own, and when they're loud, insistent, or pervasive, we can easily abandon our own rhythms. This is what drags us down in a boring lecture or ramps us up in a rock concert or sports event. And this is exactly why we go into Nature. We regain a natural rhythm when we entrain to the pace of flowing water, rustling leaves, and animals going about their business.

Start From Where You Are, Again

As we found in the introduction to the ABCs, where we are is the best place from which to start the time management journey. Although this seems self-evident, it's not what most of us do. We wish we were further along and we're ashamed or irritated that we aren't. If you acknowledge where you are, you'll have a stronger, more realistic base from which to proceed. As Parker Palmer said in an interview with Bill Moyers, "reality won't let you down."[9] You'll be grounded, steady, and realistic. From there you can take your whole self with you on the journey.

Paying attention to whatever is happening now, be it "good" or "bad," comfortable or uncomfortable, helps us become kinder to ourselves and thereby foster a helpful atmosphere in which to work. Most of us work more willingly for a kind, accepting mentor than a stern taskmaster.

Paying attention to it all also widens our view. Instead of struggling between the opposites of good and bad, comfortable and uncomfortable, we accept it all. We take in much more than before. Our world becomes larger, not so caught up in the minutiae of life.

With a measure of constancy and control of our attention, we gain an internal coherence at the center of our being. We more easily take our cues from within, rather than deferring to external authority. No longer are we at the mercy of every passing event or tossed about by surface storms. Our lives follow the slower-moving currents beneath the surface where life is less chaotic and dissatisfying, and more cohesive, resonant, and rich.

CHAPTER 5

BOUNDARIES—
PROTECTED AND
CONNECTED

Bodies have skin; cells have membranes; water droplets have sur-face tension. These containing, enveloping boundaries allow a thing to exist. Without them, there is no "thing," just an undifferen-tiated mass of stuff. With them, whatever it is can grow, flourish, and explore its unique way of being.

Time management boundaries work in much the same way. They provide a protective sac within which we discover our particular gifts, preferences, desires, and needs—what is essential for us. When we say "No," we realize that the rejected request is someone else's choice, not ours. When we say "Yes," we recall what makes our heart sing. The boundary helps us make appropriate distinctions between Me and Not Me, and so helps us remember who we are.

Boundaries Mediate Between Inside and Outside

The boundary that defines a thing also mediates between that thing and the larger world of which it is a part. Think of a cell's membrane. It not only defines the cell but allows the cell to interact with its larger environment. Through it the cell takes in nourishment and information and releases chemicals and unneeded substances.

The health of the cell depends upon the health of its semi-per-meable membrane. If something compromises that membrane, there's potential for trouble. An "unfriendly" substance could invade the cell. It might become unable to take in what it needs. It might fail to release appropriate chemicals to influence the organism. It could even lose its integrity and dissolve. A healthy membrane supports the cell's own health and, ultimately, that of the entire organism.

So it is with time management boundaries. Like those of cells, our boundaries must be permeable yet not indiscriminately open. For instance, if we habitually accommodate others' needs and ignore our own, we let in too much of what's out there and deplete our internal resources. On the other hand, if we get so caught up in our own concerns that we ignore what's going on around us, we become closed off and unable to participate in life's richness. Our world shrinks.

Of course, there are times when self-absorption is appropriate— when we're at risk or in transition. We might be sick, moving our household, getting a divorce, or pregnant. These are times when we need to focus within. At other times, accommodating others' needs is appropriate, such as when caring for small children or ailing parents.

These times pass and when they do, we can reestablish a healthy balance of inward and outward focus, which is the basis for sustainable time management. Boundaries that are firm and flexible protect and connect us. We take on some tasks, expectations, and proposals and reject others.

Core and Periphery

A reciprocal relationship exists between the internal core of our true being and the peripheral edge where we meet the world, responding and receiving. The more we trust our boundaries to filter out what we choose not to take in, the more leave we have to explore and be ourselves within the boundary. The more we say "No" (or "Yes") at the periphery, the clearer we are at our core.

In a complementary manner, the more we know ourselves, the easier it is to meet the world. As internal integrity develops, we can draw our boundary further out and take in more of the world. We widen our range, embrace a larger reality, and include more of "Them" in "Me." As we operate in a "bigger" world, we have the possibility of exerting more influence. We can make things happen as we take our special place in the interconnected web of life.

Task Boundaries—Molding Events from the River of Experience

Boundaries serve us well not just when we are choosing what to do or what not to do, but also when we are defining tasks, containing the time we spend on them, and structuring them so we can work with them more easily. Think of tasks and time as the raw material of time management, like the potter's clay. If the potter adds too much water, the clay turns into slurry and dissolves. If the potter mixes in too little water, the clay is hard and impossible to work. What the potter wants is just the right consistency—soft enough to work, firm enough to hold together. This is what we look for in time management—just enough structure but not too much.

For many of us, time seems to slip through our fingers. We rush around in furious activity but at the end of the day, what can we say we did? It's all a blur. We're swept along in the river of experience, immersed in what's happening, at the mercy of every passing demand, whether from inside ourselves or from others.

With good task boundaries, we can step out of the reactive river and take a wider view from the bank. From this vantage point, we can more easily choose one task over another. We can dive in or step out as we choose. We feel on top of things, not overwhelmed. Task boundaries contain what we do with kindly care. They protect our sometimes-vulnerable task from intrusion and allow us to work freely and safely within them.

Three-Phase Close-Down

The technique that follows is a central practice of sustainable time management—one that people report again and again has changed their lives. It offers satisfaction, flexibility, spaciousness, and a sense of engagement with how we operate moment-to-moment. It also runs directly counter to how most people do things.

For many of us, while we're doing one thing, we're thinking about the next thing. We rush headlong through a day, moving on to something else before finishing what's before us. We rarely feel satisfaction and accomplishment. Even though we do a lot, it seems like we never do enough. Does that sound familiar?

The three-phase close-down is a means to make graceful transitions between tasks. It allows us not to worry about what's next. It gives us time to acknowledge our accomplishments every step of the way, thus cultivating an encouraging sense of satisfaction. Here's how it works.

First, establish an overall time limit. For example, you might have twenty minutes before a meeting. Instead of working on a minor task that fits into the time available, you begin a major task, say a report that will take hours to complete (and that you certainly would've procrastinated on). Contain the time by setting a timer.

Don't, however, set the timer for twenty minutes. Just as it takes time for your computer to shut down, so it takes time to close down a task. Allow about a quarter to a third of the total time for close-down. Here, you would set the timer for fifteen minutes. While the timer is ticking you can work freely, intensely even, without fear of getting swallowed up by the task or needing to keep an eye on the clock.

When the alarm rings, you stop—just stop. Period. There's more where that came from, so you might as well stop now. Then, move into the close-down, which focuses on the past, the future, and the present.

The past

The first phase of the close-down is to look to the past—what just happened—and acknowledge progress thus far. In the case of the report, you may have developed the first two points and noticed that you need input from a colleague before proceeding. All of this is useful to know and worth acknowledging.

This practice of letting what we did sink in is the key point. As you saw in the previous chapter, most of us focus so much on what we still need to do that we don't notice what we have accomplished. Since there's always more to do, such an orientation sets us up for being discouraged. Or we might only give ourselves credit when we finish the whole job. Under those conditions, we get one pat on the back. That's it.

Instead, acknowledge progress early and often—every single time you work, even if only for ten minutes. "Satisfaction practice" shifts our self-concept from someone who doesn't do enough to someone who accomplishes something every time she works. Think of that! As we let what we did register, we're less worried about the final product because we see progress every step of the way. We experience a new spaciousness—contained in that fifteen minutes is a whole world, and we have protected that world from everything else. This orientation recognizes more of the reality of the situation—something did indeed happen!

The future

Next, look to the future. Write down the very next step (it might be "ask colleague for input; begin point #3"). When you come back, you can pick up right where you left off without wasting time figuring out where you were. You might also schedule the next time to take it up.

We've all had the experience of leaving a task mid-stream, coming back to it and taking fifteen minutes just to figure out where we were. By identifying the next step during the close-down, you can return to exactly where you left off and slip back into the task from there. This is very much like the Pause Button technique in the Attention chapter. You can even capture the feeling and flavor of the moment. Artists do this. In creating a work over time, they learn how to call forth the feeling as well as the stopping point.

The present

Finally, settle down the present. Gather all the papers, put the next step trigger-note on top, and move the project to the side. Now you can go to the meeting, satisfied with a job well begun, confident that you know exactly where to start again, and with a clear desk ready for whatever's next when you return.

Here's how the close-down works in practice. Say, you decide that you should really make that difficult call to the insurance company. You've been putting it off, saying, "When I'm done with the house-work, then I'll make the call." (So … when might that be???) You then say to yourself, "OK. I'll put in a ten-minute session with the insurance issue." You set the timer for seven minutes and launch in. You might gather the papers together, review them, and see what further information you need. In fact, you might not even place the call. When the timer buzzes, you move into the close-down. You let what you did do sink in, you set up the next step (perhaps schedule the call), and put it aside. You leave it gracefully, knowing that you've made a good start on a difficult task and the next step is ready for you.

How Closing Down Helps

With the close-down, our options multiply. We don't have to push through—we can stop whenever we choose. We don't have to do it for as long as it takes (whatever that is!)—we can do it for any length of time. We can honor commitments to ourselves and others without getting stuck in them.

We also gain a better sense of how to navigate through the work. I call this process alternating between eagle-view and ant-view. The eagle is above the work, surveying the whole scene. The ant is on the ground doing the work. In the close-down, we move from ant-doing to eagle-perspective. We've stepped back, yet we have stayed connected to the task. This slightly detached middle ground is a valuable place to cultivate. From here, we can more clearly perceive what's happening and gather good information to help us decide what to do next.

For example, with the insurance call, you may find out in the Past review phase of the close-down that you're great at assembling data, but not so great at synthesizing it into specific questions to ask during the call. Knowing that, your Future next step might be to ask a friend to help you think through the synthesizing process. The close-down helps you acknowledge the facts of the matter and take appropriate action.

The close-down addresses a host of time management issues like procrastination, lack of focus, doing it until it's done, doing what fits into the time available, neglecting what we need to do for what we like to do, and feeling overwhelmed. Here's how.

Procrastination

Resisting action is as complex as it is common. We might procrastinate because we hate filing papers. Or maybe we feel burdened by the enormous task of doing our taxes. We might even feel oppressed by the consequences of figuring out our purpose in life. So we procrastinate. It makes perfect sense.

Here's how the close-down helps. First, it limits the time we spend on a task. If we know we're only going to do a task for fifteen minutes, we can start it more easily. We're only dipping a toe into the pool of the task. Then, using the close-down, we acknowledge (and celebrate) that we were able to get into it at all, set up an easy way to get back in, and beat a quick retreat. Phew!

Second, the close-down softens the boundary between us and the task. Instead of the task boundary being a brick wall, there's a window to peek in, or even a door to walk through. We can get into those big tasks, like deciding to change jobs, without going on a weekend retreat— although the retreat might be just the thing!

Third, setting a time limit stokes the white heat of a deadline to motivate us to action. With the close-down, we have a back boundary to bump up against. We've all experienced meetings where nothing happens until the last ten minutes, when the end looms and people get down to business. We can do the same with tasks. Setting a back boundary helps the work heat up nicely. (Of course, we need to honor our own deadline, but this gets easier with practice.)

Lack of focus

Task boundaries that are too soft compromise focus. We can't quite decide what to do, so we putter around and do lots of little things. This is fine as long as there's not some big task to do. When we can't seem to engage with what's before us all we may need to do is set a time limit. Working within a boundary sharpens our focus.

Doing it until it's done

We often allow the task to set the boundary rather than setting it ourselves, saying, "I'll do it till it's done." If we habitually operate this way, it's easy to neglect other important tasks, get over-absorbed in one task, exhaust ourselves, and fritter away time, especially towards the end of the task. Setting a task boundary allows us to steer our own ship. We do the task for a while, then stop, acknowledge progress, re-strategize, review how it's going, and get back to it later with fresh energy. And we get satisfaction every step of the way, not just when we finish the task.

Doing what fits into the time available

Rarely do we have acres of time stretching out before us. Most often, it's a snippet here and a moment there, which sets up a kind of reverse procrastination. We do whatever happens to fit into that bit of free time, saying, "Oh, I'll just do this little thing now and cross it off my list." There's nothing wrong with that intrinsically—we can get a lot of little things done—but when we neglect the big things and busy ourselves with the little things, there's a problem. Most of the projects that feed the cores of our beings don't fit into little snippets, and those little tasks that do fit never end! Changing this pattern helps us get to the heart of things and do what's important.

Neglecting what we need to do for what we want to do

Just as we avoid doing things we don't like, we can also pour pitchers of time into things we do like. With the close-down we can give quality time to cherished tasks while not neglecting other urgent and important matters. In each session, we let the satisfaction of doing what we love reverberate. We don't miss those good feelings.

Feeling overwhelmed

The complexity and scope of a big task can stop us dead in our tracks. Short sessions help us gingerly get into the big project. Our first session may be nothing more than taking a general view and figuring out where to start. In another short session, we might plan how to navigate through the work. Then, after these initial forays, we launch into the big task, again in short sessions, acknowledging progress as we go. (Look to Part IV—the Resource section for a technique for breaking down complex projects into chewable chunks.)

Variations On a Theme

Since the three-phase close-down runs counter to most people's usual way of operating, it would be wise to practice it just as it is for a while so you'll have a reliable new tool in your toolbox, a different way of operating to pull out when appropriate. That said, in certain situations, you may find that variations on the three-phase theme work well.

Continuing after a close-down

As you step back from the work and take a wider view in the close-down, you see that your energy is still flowing and there are no other tasks tugging at your attention. You decide that it's actually appropriate to continue. This is fine as long as you avoid falling into the "do it till it's done" pattern where you work to exhaustion or neglect other important tasks.

Start-up as well as close-down

Sometimes you need to take time to get into a task, as well as to get out of it. When this is the case, set a timer for start-up as well as close-down. This technique is especially useful when you're doing something you've never done before or a task is complex. A start-up session, separated from the actual doing, can make the task less daunting.

Mozart and multi-tasking

The classic close-down applies to one task at a time (and indeed, it's worthwhile to get good at that). However, the close-down can work when there are several tasks open at once—multi-tasking. Although this word has gotten a lot of attention, the fact remains that we actually do one thing at a time. What passes as multi-tasking is, in fact, rapid switching between several tasks. This is fine for tasks that don't require deep concentration, creative reflection, or sustained attention. The trick is to take plenty of time to close down all the active tasks in the multi-task arena. You have to screw the lids back on all the cans of worms you've opened.

Mozart's music offers an apt metaphor for multi-tasking. He had an extremely fertile, active musical mind—some say he was the original ADD-guy! Ideas come tumbling onto the score, one after another. This feels like the way I clean house. I get out the ironing board, then run a sink of dishwater, pull out the mop bucket, get the silver polish, and throw a load in the washer. Over the course of the morning, I switch between laundry, dishes, floors, polishing silver, and whatever else I'm into that day.

Mozart's like that. He gets a whole bunch of musical ideas going, and plays with them over the course of the movement. About two-thirds of the way in, however, he starts to end—a classic close-down. In that final third, themes repeat for the last time, little fragments get bundled in with bigger themes, high notes and low notes come back to the home key, so that by the time you get to the closing chords there's a satisfying Aaah. Everything is sewn up in a ball.

This is not random bouncing around, but rather conscious attention to one line of activity within the larger space of other activities. When you're conscious of all the parts within the whole, and close them all down, at the end of the morning there's a satisfying Aaah as you survey the refreshed scene. Just make sure you allow plenty of time for close-down!

Transitions

As we shape experience with task boundaries we get better information. We feel less overwhelmed. We feel more satisfied. All of this sounds wonderful. Yet we resist. We balk at time constraints, we abhor deadlines, and we don't want to beat the clock. Why not? One mostly unacknowledged reason is that when tasks are discrete, we have to make formal, conscious transitions from one task to the next, and transitions are scary. When we immerse ourselves in a task without boundaries, we feel connected, engaged, and responsive. That sounds great. Still, we will have to stop and transition to something else at some point. How do we do that? Crossing over from the familiar to the unknown is not easy.

Many cultures acknowledge the delicacy of transitions and the vulnerable state we're in as we make them with special ceremonies—initiations, weddings, funerals. Ancient traditions have special deities worshipped at boundaries and borders—Hermes, his more ancient counterpart, Terminus, and Hecate.

Transitions are formidable, yet we do them all the time. Take getting out of bed. There we are, held in comfortable warmth, drifting in dreamland. Consider what we ask of ourselves—exposing ourselves to cold, becoming vulnerable to outside influences, having to

DO something. And what will that something be? What will the day bring? No wonder we resist.

Yet, when we're actually up, things aren't so bad. It's a beautiful day. We're open to surprises, new stimuli, connection with the world, challenges that stretch us. We feel alive and growing. But tell me that when I'm in bed. None of the benefits are guaranteed. The weather could turn; I could make a mistake; I could get hurt, embarrassed, or discouraged. No thank you, I'll stay right here where it's warm and comfy. This is where special techniques and tools come in handy—like alarm clocks.

When we're about to cross into a new task, distressing emotions can arise. We feel ashamed that we haven't already finished what we're just beginning. Or we're embarrassed to have done only a fraction of what we'd expected. Or we're leaving familiar territory and have to figure out what's next. No wonder we have trouble with transitions.

It's helpful to acknowledge how scary this in-between place really is. As forward-facing, upright beings, we are poised to go forth, but to do so we can use all the help we can get. The three-phase closedown offers the time and technique we need. We also need kindness and courage to make the transition, calling on internal and external allies—who you'll meet in the chapter on Change—to help us through this No-Man's Land. As we get better at transitions, our anxiety won't be so protracted or deep. We'll be able to move gracefully from task to task with satisfaction and confidence.

Personal Boundaries

Good personal boundaries make all of this much easier. Like the cell mentioned at the start of this chapter, each of us is a unit, defined most obviously by the boundary of our skin. We have a sense of where "I" end and "The Other Out There" begins. Appropriate interactions with everyone and everything "Out There" depend on the health of our boundaries. As with the semi-permeable membrane of the cell, boundaries that are firm (not rigid) and flexible (not flabby) keep in what's good and keep out what's not so good.

Replenishing Resources

When we have plenty of what's good—a full complement of resources upon which to draw—we can interact most appropriately with the world. Many of us, however, in our fast-paced, stimulus-laden, demanding environment operate on empty. We're chronically depleted, worn out, and weary. So we need to replenish ourselves regularly. Like the lady of the manor who holds the store-house keys and ensures the castle is well-provisioned, we need to make sure our resource banks are full, and with the right stuff.

We need to know in detail what sustains and nourishes us. It may be good food, refreshing rest, mental stimulus, satisfying emotional contact, connection with the natural world, connection to the source of our being, physical challenge. Each of us is unique. Some people like a sweaty workout; others enjoy quiet strolling. Some like to experience an emotional release; others prefer journal writing. It's helpful to think of resources in four areas—physical, emotional, mental, and spiritual. Here are a few activities to help you replenish your resources in each area. Let them stimulate you to come up with a list of your own. Include activities that don't require special equipment, particular conditions, or a lot of time, so that when you have only a few moments, you can choose an appropriate activity from your list.

Physical replenishment

Both rest and activity replenish our reserves. Something as simple as walking around the block may do the trick for you. Or, maybe you enjoy a yoga class, working out at the gym, eating healthy food, or getting a full night's rest. Even taking a conscious breath can replenish you physically. Breathing takes no special equipment, you can do it anywhere, it takes only a few moments, and no one needs to know you're doing it. The benefits far outweigh the effort involved.

Emotional replenishment

Replenishing emotional resources often comes through others. You might call a friend, spend time with a child, or pet a dog. You might listen to music that matches your mood. You might "recharge" yourself emotionally by focusing on life's blessings and feeling gratitude. Or having a good cry. Or a good laugh! Or encountering beauty in some form and letting it move you.

Mental replenishment

Both stimulus and relaxation can replenish exhausted mental resources. You might do a crossword puzzle or play a game of chess—games operate in a playing arena outside our usual mind patterns and so can be relaxing as well as stimulating. Or, you might read for pleasure, or learn something new. For some, a healthy political wrangle refreshes; for others, emptying the mind with meditation does the job.

Spiritual replenishment

Spiritual replenishment often comes from reestablishing a connection to the divine, to the source of our being. To do so, you might pray, take a nature walk, read spiritually-oriented literature, or participate in a religious gathering of any sort. When you consciously do activities in seemingly non-spiritual areas, you can also reestablish this connection—eat a conscious meal, take a conscious breath, enjoy a conscious laugh, and have a conscious political wrangle!

Replenishing resources is a daily practice, not a once-and-for-all business. We can't say, "Oh, I'll breathe on Saturday"; we have to breathe every day, every moment. Each day we need the nourishment, repair, and rest these activities provide, and we need at least one in each area every day. Using task boundaries and the close-down technique, we can claim time for replenishment, even if for only a brief spell.

Boundary Challenges

The old saying, "good fences make good neighbors" has some real truth to it. We know that a reliable boundary allows us to be ourselves. Protected within, we can become ever more who we really are and develop our internal integrity. Yet we want to feel at one with our fellows, held in the embrace of community. This is a basic human need. So our challenge is to stay protected and connected. Think of the king, at the center of the realm, protected by border guards. The guards are reliable and well-trained. They make sure unwanted invaders don't slip in, yet they allow for free passage of friendly visitors. So it is with our boundaries. We need to have them in place so we can meet the challenges that come inevitably.

Feelings point to the middle way

Other people challenge our boundaries all the time—a coworker barges in with a new agenda, a child wants lunch NOW, Aunt Martha calls with excruciating details of her aches and pains. When that happens to us, a wide range of emotions arise. We feel angry, frustrated, and aggressive, or overwhelmed, guilty, and confused. In the case of anger, frustration, and aggression, our boundaries grow spikes—we want to overpower the intruder or dismiss them. In the case of feeling overwhelmed, guilty, or confused, our boundaries go to mush—we give in or withdraw.

It works best if we can develop a middle way. Instead of pushing, we step back and soften our boundary to include the intruder. We acknowledge that the other person has a point—what they're asking seems perfectly reasonable to them. We give them some space, although we may not ultimately agree with them or do what they ask. On the other side, instead of caving in, we hold our ground. We might ask for time to think it over so we can establish a clearer connection with our inner self and protect ourselves behind a firm boundary. We take some space.

When we operate in this middle way, we neither overpower nor withdraw. Other people's agendas don't suck us in, yet we remain open to others' ideas. There's equal pressure from the inside and the outside. We acknowledge both sides of the issue—yours and mine. As you began to explore in the previous chapter, good time management depends on finding a way to live gracefully in this both/and (not either/or) place. American society, with its emphasis on independence (each person has their own house, car, washing machine, lawn mower, etc.), disposes us to be not so used to the both/and way. The more we maintain a boundary that's neither prickly nor punky, spiky nor squishy, the better we can operate.

Expand or contract

We draw our boundaries closer in or move them farther out as the context requires. Here's what happened to me one Sunday of a glorious holiday weekend. I had spent Saturday in the open awareness of "walkabout," traveling alone, with boundaries wide open. I had hoped to continue that mood through Sunday. However, I found myself on a popular trail where it soon became clear that yesterday's mood was not today's. Troop after troop of noisy walkers who seemed to have no appreciation for their lovely surroundings marched by.

I tried to come up with an appropriate boundary mode. If I wasn't going to do "open awareness," then I'd do "meet & greet connection." That got thwarted, too. Some folks responded, and others didn't. I needed to stay true to myself and only connect as appropriate with each passing party. With some folks I was warm and cordial, with others there was only a nod.

When we're among friends or in familiar, trustworthy circumstances, we let our boundaries expand. When we're in unknown territory—among strangers or in unusual circumstances—we draw them in. If we find ourselves habitually withdrawing, we need to make sure our range of operation doesn't narrow each time we withdraw. Those who are caught in withdrawal find it less and less possible to be themselves in company. The trick is to both connect to our inner selves and to venture forth. When we do this our world becomes bigger, more inclusive. We're more creative, more powerful.

On my square

Boundary challenges don't just come from outside. Often they come from within. In one martial arts move, you stretch out your arms laterally as you move side to side. I'm pretty flexible, so I can extend myself quite a bit. My teacher, however, reined me in. I was going too far. Although I could stretch quite a ways, I was going far beyond where my center could hold.

This is a pattern for me, and for many people who are capable, eager, and willing to do what they feel they need to do. We extend ourselves far beyond our capacity to hold the center. Physically this could manifest as exhaustion, arthritis, all kinds of joint problems, and difficulties with the limbs. The teacher recommended limiting my reach to as far as my least able limb could go. That way I could take my whole self with me as I moved. We need to "stay on our square"—acknowledge yet not fall prey to others' expectations and obligations, remember that we have needs, and keep a strong connection with our inner core.

A Conduit for the Energy of Life

A sound pipeline gives enough structural integrity to contain whatever flows through it. If it rusts through or breaks, it ceases to be of use. Similarly, the firm banks of a fast-flowing stream contain the water as it rushes through so that the water might even power a mill. If the banks cave in, however, the water becomes muddy. It might even spread out and become stagnant like a swamp.

Personal boundaries are like that. Enveloping us in their protective sac, they provide a conduit for the energy of life flowing through us. If the boundaries are healthy, we can use our power effectively. If they're leaky, our power dissipates. We have to work too hard to do what we want to do—if we get anything done at all!

It's good to remember that healthy boundaries not only protect us (and the energy flowing through us), they also connect us to the wider world. With a good boundary we can meet the world and influence it for the greater good of all, ourselves included!

CHAPTER 6

CHOICES—IN TUNE
WITH SELF AND
OTHERS

M aking a choice is where time management really begins to
show. Should I write the report or respond to the e-mail?
Should I pick up the laundry or take a walk? Should I clean my desk
or make the phone call? Should I stop or should I continue? Making
choices (and taking action on behalf of those choices) is where the
time management rubber meets the road.

Choices are particularly fraught. Either we seem to have too many
choices or no choice at all. "Having too many choices," says Barry
Schwartz in his book, *The Paradox of Choice*, "produces psychological
distress, especially when combined with regret, concern about sta-
tus, adaptation, social comparison, and perhaps most important, the
desire to have the best of everything."[10] On the other hand, how
often do we say, "I don't have a choice" when obligations weigh us
down?

Conscious or Not?

Implicit in our very natures as self-conscious, freestanding beings is
a kind of free will. (Compared to the rest of creation—animals and
plants, for example—it's a considerable level of free will!) Viktor
Frankl points out in *Man's Search for Meaning* that even in a concentration camp, a most constrained and horrific situation, we have a
choice about how to respond, what to think, even how to feel.[11]
Although the surrounding environment, be it a traditional culture,

Frankl's concentration camp, a desert island, or twenty-first century America, has a whole set of "givens" where there seems to be no choice, we can choose, at every moment, what to do and how to do it.

Even though we could make all these choices, for the most part, choices just seem to happen. We're not particularly aware of having made them. We're distracted by a "squeaky wheel," so we "oil" it by doing what it asks. We have only a certain amount of time available, so we do whatever happens to fit into it. An uncomfortable task confronts us, so we avoid it. We feel burdened by endless expectations so we do what we want, rather than what we should. Conversely, if we feel guilty about taking time for ourselves, we do what's expected.

Such less-than-fully conscious choices can get us into trouble. We do what's not so important or neglect what is. We burn out and fall ill. We feel we're missing out on life and get resentful. In the long run, this way of operating serves neither ourselves nor the greater good.

As you saw in the opening chapter, it's impossible to do it all. And so we must choose, and we do choose, all the time. It would be better all around if we made our choices more consciously. Then we could stand behind them. We could embrace the limits of time and space—welcome to Planet Earth—with grace and good humor.

From Flat to Perspective

Take a look at the following string of words:

that that that is is that that that is not is not is not that it it is

As it stands, it makes no sense, but when we punctuate it, the words come into relationship with one another.

That that that is, is; that that that is not, is not—is not that it? It is!

Instead of the words following one after another in a procession, we bring some words to the foreground while letting others fall into the background. We establish relationships that show some words as more central than others. Thus the string of words becomes meaningful.

Choosing among time management tasks can work in a similar way. Instead of one task following the next, and the next, and the next, in an endless procession, we give some tasks more weight and others less. We say "Yes" to some things and "No" to others. We establish relationships among them.

The skills in the previous chapters help us make such choices more easily. Attention skills establish a steady enough core of internal attention to center us within ourselves. With self-awareness, we can know better what we want. Good personal boundary skills help us protect this knowledge so that we take both ourselves and others into account when making a choice. Task boundary skills make the tasks discrete enough so it's possible to choose among them. By parceling out time with task boundaries, we can let the time we spend at a task reflect its importance to us.

Start Here and Ripple Out

Many people (especially women) automatically put others first. They think of what the family needs, what the company wants, or what society expects rather than what they truly desire. There's nothing wrong with that—all of us want to participate in something larger than ourselves. The trouble comes when we become overly dependent on what's "out there" and ignore what's "in here"—our own good instincts. We neglect the connection to inner sources of vitality, peace, and joy. In so doing, we lose our center and cease making our unique contribution to the world. For our own health, as well as for the growth and evolution of the world, we need to put ourselves into the mix when making choices.

So in this chapter, as in the two before, your initial focus will be on making good choices for yourself. You'll come to know what you choose for yourself—and then ripple out to include others in your choice-making.

Choose What Feels Good

In the first phase of the close-down practice in the Boundaries chapter, you learned how good it can feel to acknowledge what we accomplish—what helped, what got you somewhere. As it turns out, attention to what feels good can be the single criterion to use for any choice—does it feel good or does it feel bad? Is it healthy, life-promoting, encouraging, or satisfying? Or is it draining, demoralizing, deadly, off-kilter, or dissatisfying? That's it.

It may take some doing to discern what "good" actually feels like. Our tendency is to look for clues as to what's good outside of us—to family, peers, community, society in general. Of course, the commercial media has no problem telling us in detail what's good, just as long as we buy whatever it is they're hawking.

Our practice here, however, is to sensitize our antennae to the good feelings that bubble up from within. Say, you're pleased to have taken the first baby-step on a dreaded task—that's good. Your warmed-up body tells you that the walk around the block released tension—that's good. You're relieved to have answered the sensitive letter that's been hanging around for weeks—that's good.

We get better at recognizing the feelings, based on the body, intuition, and heart as much as reason, which naturally tell us what's good. At first, there may seem to be only a tiny shred of "good" in what we did. However, instead of saying, "It's *only just* this good," we say, "It's good." Period.

Focus on the good establishes a direction to follow and generates an inclination to follow it. In physics, this is called a vector—a pull in a particular direction. Leaning into the positive, we establish a relationship with it, an affinity, a sympathy, a magnetism. We set up a situation where we're drawn to what we choose. It's alluring, enticing, inviting, fascinating, captivating, and appealing. These good feelings gently encourage us to choose well.

The Cascade of Implications

We do have to watch out, however, for a domino effect that can happen when we go with what's good. For example, if you say "Yes" to going skiing, then you may feel like you have to say "Yes" to taking winter trips, investing in particular equipment, or hanging out with certain people. We need to realize that saying "Yes" to one thing doesn't imply an automatic "Yes" to everything that follows.

This scenario recalls step-by-step consent in sexual relationships that many college campuses instituted to address date-rape. Whoever was "making a move" had to ask "Is it all right if I do this?" at every step along the way. Saying "Yes" to the kiss doesn't imply saying "Yes" to intercourse. With time management, there's a choice every step along the way. You can always back out; you can always say "No." I remember the first time (not too long ago) that I didn't eat the whole candy bar. I bought it, had a few delicious bites, wanted no more, and threw the rest of the bar away. Imagine that!

Negative Navigation

Often we make choices by avoiding nasty things, rather than by going towards good things. This puts us in the position of "navigating negatively." We're exquisitely tuned into what seems bad in order to get away from it or blot it out. This orientation is certainly necessary at times, but for many of us, the orientation is habitual. We spend our lives avoiding unpleasantness. The truth of the matter is that every situation has both "good" and "bad" aspects to it, so focusing on the good rights the balance, allowing us to see both sides of the situation. As you'll see in the next chapter on Change, even what seems "bad" can be good.

Feel Good Practice

To get a better handle on how you actually feel about things, you might want to get a "witness," a friend with whom to talk about what feels good. Or you might keep a journal and list ten things every day that you like (or don't like!). In fact, at the beginning, it's often easier to know what doesn't feel good. At least it's a place to start.

Stephen Buhner in his book, *Secret Teachings of Plants*,[12] suggests a practice of going on an attraction walk each day. Walk down a street and notice what draws your attention, what you like. Make note of it—remember the shop window, the display of red peppers in the supermarket. Let your desire present itself.

Sometimes it's hard to know in advance what we would like. If this happens to you, it might be helpful to make a To Do list in the morning, then not look at it until the end of the day. As you reflect on what happened, get a sense of what drew you to those tasks you did and what turned you away from those you thought you wanted to do and didn't. Use this information to get more of the good stuff and use your skills (especially task boundary skills) to deal with the bad stuff. Or, as you make your morning list, play out each option in your imagination. Notice which options feel good and which feel bad, which options attract you and which repel you.

More on Feelings

In order to choose based on how things feel, we need access to feelings just as they are—all of them. Books like *Emotional Intelligence*, *Emotional Genius*, and various personal growth processes, trainings, and therapies offer systems, insights, and practices to become more aware and accepting of emotions. (See Part IV, the Resource section for some possibilities.) Most of these systems advise that we acknowledge feelings but not let our feelings swallow us up—somewhat like how we encounter the weather.

The weather is the weather. It is the way it is, and it changes. We can feel upset or happy about the weather, but there it is—rain or shine. With our feeling life, we can feel good or bad, or we can simply name what's happening now. It is what it is. Whether we feel good or bad can be valuable information when we're making time management choices.

Sometimes life deposits us in a place where feelings seem to have disappeared. Who knows if we feel good—or bad, for that matter? It's like grey, soft weather where there's no perceivable sun in the sky. Feelings are gone, dissolved, dissipated; they've lost their energy and power. Sometimes this emotional non-weather passes on its own; other times we're stuck in it.

Parker Palmer's *Let Your Life Speak* has a courageous account of major depression. When we're cut off from the sources of our vitality there's a temptation to go to stimulants, personal drama, over-busy-ness, or other forms of denial. These strategies may seem to rouse us, but they have their own consequences and often don't really get us moving.

When there seems to be no draw or pull, the options from which to choose often aren't attractive—there's no traction, no vector. In such situations, you might have to make space to notice the stirrings and wait for attraction to present itself. This is where a good friend, therapist, or other witness can help you. Somehow, and it's a mystery, really, if you keep making space, the pull will come back. It happens less by will than by presence, patience, and kindliness towards oneself.

Choosing Shows Us Who We Are

As we pay attention to where we're drawn, the pressure between the inside and the outside equalizes. External forces become less compelling; internal authority becomes clearer and stronger. We become free agents, no longer slaves to others' expectations and external obligations. As we come to know what we really want and make our choices on that basis, what we do reflects who we are.

This process is gloriously self-reinforcing. As we sense where we're drawn and act accordingly, we see the results of our actions before us. We clearly see what we want. Acting on our desires makes our desires clearer. Our will and life purpose become manifest. We take our place in the world with confidence and clarity.

Challenges to Choosing

It's no surprise that choosing is a challenge. Here are three major difficulties in making a choice: first, there are complex factors to sort out, including those involving others; second, we want whatever choice we make to be the right choice; and third, we'd rather not have to choose at all—we want to do everything! Here are some practices and insights to help.

Untangling the Factors

A whole host of factors are involved in making a time management choice. Most often, they're all tangled up. One item may be important, but it takes a lot of time. Another is easy, but might not have a lot of effect. Another happens to fit into the time available, but feels too demanding.

Here are the major factors involved. Considering them one by one gives us better information on which to base the choice.

Importance—Does this task have weight? Will it have a lot of effect throughout the system in which it is embedded? Is it in line with my mission or any mission I've taken on?

Urgency—Do I need to do this task now or soon in order for it to be worthwhile? Is it time-sensitive? Will doing it later hamper other people or processes down the line?

Attraction—Is this task something I want to do? Does it draw me, even though it may be difficult or time-consuming? Does it bring out the best in me?

Benefit—Will doing this task make things easier, more effective, or better in any way for myself or others? Will doing it ripple out in helpful, positive ways? Will it have a good effect in the long run?

Quick and easy

There are two more factors on which we often base our choices—quick and easy. How many times have you heard yourself say, "Oh, that won't take much time; I'll just do it and get it off my list" or "Oh, that's easy, I can do that." There's nothing wrong with doing the quick and easy, as long as those tasks have some of the other four factors, especially importance. If we default to the quick and easy, we'll find ourselves crossing lots of insignificant things off our lists and never getting to important things that aren't so quick and easy.

The three-phase close-down is the great equalizer of the quick factor. You learned in the last chapter that even huge projects that take hours can happen in small chunks of time. In fact, that's the only way huge projects actually happen. Think of the violinist who wants to play the Beethoven Violin Concerto. He can't just practice until he gets it and play it in one session. It takes many, many sessions of practice over weeks, months, and even years of time. This isn't quick.

To equalize the easy factor, we tease out the components of a daunting project and deconstruct them into tasks that we can actually do easily. A practice for doing this appears in Part IV, the Resource section. The small task is connected to the whole, so by doing it we are actually working on the huge task (think Beethoven Violin Concerto). When closing down a session with a daunting task, be sure to identify a next step that's easy. Then you can slip right back in next time.

The untangling game

Here is a little game to untangle the factors involved in a choice. Take six tasks from your To Do list that you really think you should do and write them on 3x5 cards—one task per card.

First, give each task an Importance rating on a 1 to 10 scale, with 10 being most important. Note the rating in the upper right corner of the card. Be sure this is an Importance rating, not an Urgency rating (we'll get to that later).

Now, completely ignoring the Importance factor, give each task an Urgency rating, again 1 to 10 with 10 being the most urgent. Note the Urgency rating in the upper left corner.

Next, consider Attraction—how much do you want to do this? Give the things you love to do a 10, and give the things you hate to do a 1. Note that rating in the lower right corner.

Finally, give the task a Benefit rating from 10 (lots of benefit now and into the future for the widest range of people and situations) to 1 (inconsequential in the long run).

When all the ratings are 6 or above (it's fairly important, urgent, attractive, and beneficial), you're going to do it. This is a no-brainer. When most of the scores are low—it's not so important, doesn't give a lot of benefit, and you hate doing it—this is also a no-brainer. Don't do it!

You'll face difficulties when there's a wide disparity between the numbers, say, 9 on Importance and 1 on Attraction. For example, you need to publicize an important event. To do so, you have to call a lot of people you don't know and you hate making cold calls. Here are ways to help.

> Contain the time you spend on the task by using a timer and the close-down—most people can do just about anything, even the most repulsive task, for fifteen minutes.

> Get help—take some training or delegate the task to someone who likes that sort of thing.

> Adjust your expectations and don't take it personally—you're lousy at PR, but you're great at other tasks.

Many tasks are high on Importance or Benefit and low on Urgency—like figuring out your life purpose or revamping your file system. You need to get going on those tasks regardless. Crowbar in a short session—even ten minutes—and close down well. Acknowledge your progress no matter how small; identify the next step and schedule another session; and finally, put the task aside so you can cleanly get back to those more urgent matters. It's wonderfully satisfying and calming to take up an important task that's been on the back burner for a long time. Once you try it, you'll probably want to do more of it!

Wanting to Do It Right

It's no surprise that we want to "do it right," considering all the messages we get, especially from commercial media. We see fabulous celebrities, and even ordinary people, doing it right at every turn. After all, that's news, and it sells. In order to avoid the shame and discouragement that comes when we compare our puny efforts with what we see around us, we might think we'd better not do anything unless it's "right." This can lead to an addiction to perfection.

Because we have in-your-face access to these high performers, standards of quality have flown through the roof. Anything less than 100% feels inadequate. In our comparative, competitive, commercial environment, we're always striving, never satisfied. This can lead to serious time management trouble. Remember the adage—"perfection is the enemy of production." If you wait until it's perfect, you won't get it out at all. Newspaper writers on deadline all know, "go with what you've got." The fact is most of us are intelligent, capable, and good at what we do. Operating at 85–90% is perfectly adequate to the job.

Here's a way of thinking about quality levels that may soften up perfection addiction. The basic level is Business-As-Usual, the 85% "cruising altitude" where we operate most of the time. Occasionally, when there are plenty of resources—plenty of time, plenty of money, plenty of people-power—we hit the Bells-and-Whistles 100% level. That's rare (and an occasion for a celebration, I'd say). Conversely, when resources are short—a project of greater priority intrudes or resources dwindle—we default to the Quick-and-Dirty level—the minimum to do if we're going to do it at all. When a project starts, it's smart to identify the Quick-and-Dirty level—the bare bones that will give us most of what we're looking for. Then, even though we'll be operating Business-As-Usual, we'll have a back-up plan.

Of course, we strive for quality. We want our lives to be just great! Having been a classical music critic, I know about top-notch quality—a performance where the notes are just a means of expressing the depth and complexity of the human condition. That's quality, and it's rare. A player can, nonetheless, make every moment, every note, good (not just good enough, but good). This kind of quality comes not in comparison to an objective standard but from the quality of attention brought to the enterprise. And that's within our control. We can bring quality attention to any task and be perfectly satisfied with a job imperfectly done. The internal challenge is to both accept ourselves and reach for something greater—acceptance without resignation, striving without being heartless.

Loosening our grip on what's "right"

Often we think we know what the right choice is. But our particular experience, our history, and our way of perceiving all guide our choices. Whether from "inside" ourselves, or from "outside" sources, we recognize only what we recognize. The rest (of which there is considerable) goes unnoticed. Are we sure we always know what's best?

We've all had the experience of wanting something to go one way, not having that happen, and then having the actual outcome turn out much better than we could have imagined. For example, I'd planned a particular arrival time for getting downtown. Everything conspired to make me late. Yet, just when I arrived, I saw an old friend and mentor crossing the street. I had no idea he was in town. Had I been on time I would've missed a delightful visit with him. If we insist on doing what we think is right, we can miss out on wonderful, unanticipated opportunities.

It can be an eye-opener to put choice in the hands of some kind of "chance operation." For example, you might flip a coin to determine what to do next on your list, and do it, regardless. Many people who interpret astrological charts, cast runes, or consult I Ching consider these processes not as chance, but as a means of opening a channel for information to come through that's beyond what we already know.

As we open up, we loosen the vise-grip on our plan. We cast our net and see what swims in. Sometimes we discover that so-called wrong choices can be just right. For example, we see how much we enjoy playing with a dog and how much energy it gives us (even though it's low on the priority list), or we see how much we really hate doing our taxes and decide to hand the job over to someone else.

Having to Say "No" in Order to Say "Yes"

The biggest challenge when choosing is saying "No." With a range of choices before us, the moment we say "Yes" to one of them, we have, de facto, said "No" to all the others. Can we do that? Can we really let go of all those other options?

In my seminars we do a challenge exercise to explore the feelings that arise when we have to say "No." We use the list of issues participants bring to the seminar for the Choice challenge—too much to do, procrastination, a life out of balance, constant interruptions, etc. It's a long list!

First, we choose one issue to work on—which in itself is difficult enough! Then the choice challenge begins by invoking our imagination to envision the issue completely resolved. In that state of Issue Resolved, we brainstorm the uncomfortable feelings that arise in that state, and arise they do! As it turns out, having exactly what we say we want isn't an unmitigated good.

For example, we might be working with procrastination. We'd rather not procrastinate, right? But think—if suddenly we weren't procrastinating, then what? We would have to face up to the quality of the output, which might not be as great as expected. We might not get to do other, more pleasant things. We wouldn't have a convenient, all-purpose excuse for the lack of delivery. Or in a funny way, we might feel like we've relinquished control, since we're no longer "sitting on" the project. So, it's no surprise we can't just stop procrastinating. In order to change, we need to make peace with the old patterns and leave them behind. To say "Yes" to the new way we need to say "No" to the old.

The patterns we say we would like to change keep us protected and comfortable. They keep us in a familiar groove (familiar not just to ourselves but also to others). They're a hedge against failure (how embarrassing that would be), or a hedge against success (if I succeed they'll pile on more work!).

In many instances, we may find that indeed we don't really need to give up that old way—we can build some of it into the new way. In the procrastination example, we can cultivate satisfaction with whatever level of quality we produce. We can do some of those pleasant things anyway (especially using the three-phase closedown). We can find plenty of excuses besides procrastination. We can maintain control by establishing check-ins with others involved in the project. We can learn how to ward off more work should we succeed. We can keep others in the loop about the new way so they don't get upset with the change. For the most part it's the fear of giving up the old way rather than the actuality that keeps us in the unhelpful pattern.

Saying "No" is difficult, yet we know it's good. Think of a garden—we have to weed to give the vegetables we want room to grow. Or when refining metal, we have to get rid of cubic yards of dirt to get that lovely, shiny nugget. A long-standing time management principle called The 80/20 Rule says that in any collection of items, 80% of the significance resides in 20% of the stuff. There are a few items that are really important and many that are not. Our task is to identify that 20% that's the gold, say "Yes" to that, and say "No" to the rest.

Both / And Balance

The best choices come from that delicate balance point where we serve others, *and* we take care of ourselves. We strive for excellence, *and* we accept things as they are. When we find that sweet spot, it feels really good—it's deeply satisfying to acknowledge both our individuality and our place in the web of life. As we've found earlier, it's not an either/or proposition; rather both/and.

As with boundaries, both firmness and flexibility serve us well. Say, you've decided to start work on your taxes. Instead of caving in to the ringing phone, the urge to run an errand, fatigue, or even straightening the desk (a nasty task, perhaps, but certainly less horrendous than doing taxes), you remain firm in your resolve. But, you also need to be flexible. When your friend calls and invites you on an excursion on a lovely Saturday, you set aside your plan to clean out your files and accept. How appropriate. Consider how it might have gone. Clinging too tightly to your plan, you would've missed the camaraderie and pleasure of the day.

A Technique for Achieving Balance

Here is a method to balance daily activities. It's freely adapted from Kurt Leland's book, *Menus for Impulsive Living*.[13]

Group the tasks on your To Do list into six categories—Work, Play, Body, Soul, Cycles, and Surprises.

> *Work* activities contribute to your engaged presence in the world. The most obvious is a job (paid or not).

> *Play* activities offer simple enjoyment or opportunities to experiment with life—watching a movie or acting in a play lets you "try on" different feelings.

Body activities promote physical flexibility, strength, coordination, and body awareness—walking, working out, a martial arts DVD, or yoga class.

Soul activities promote self-awareness, personal growth and inter-relationship—journaling, attending church services, dream interpretation.

Cycles activities recur on a regular basis—doing laundry, buying a car, brushing teeth.

Surprises activities are, by definition, unexpected—who knows!

The guideline is to do task sessions in each category every day and to mix them up within the day. For example, rather than doing several sessions of *Work* tasks, switch to *Body* (or some other area) before doing another session of *Work* tasks. This loosens up the tendency to devote so much time to any one category that you neglect the others. The sessions don't have to be long. For example, using the three-phase close-down technique, you can sneak in a short spell of *Body* activity—like climbing stairs or walking around the building—to break up the day.

The Greater Good of All

We've concentrated on choosing for ourselves up to this point. Now we turn to a wider view—to make choices that serve the greater good of all. Such choices align with the sustainability principle of enhancing life. When we live this way, we rest in conscious commitment, knowing that every choice serves. Fulfilling commitments to family, friends, and ever larger circles of community gives a sense of belonging, of contributing to the whole.

It sounds wonderful to enhance life, belonging, and contributing. But commitment? Hmm. We've got plenty of commitments already—to jobs, children, friends, and all the imperatives we've internalized from the surrounding culture. We can't possibly commit to more. Sure, we want to engage and participate, but commit?

What makes commitment possible are the Attention and Boundary skills from previous chapters. With a core of internal attention, we have a strong enough sense of self and individual will so that our own agenda isn't co-opted. With firm, yet flexible boundaries we're protected from automatic obligations and don't get pulled apart. We become sovereign beings participating in the web of mutual obligations and interconnections that makes life rich and satisfying.

The Holon

A current systems model is that of the holon. In it, each part is a whole in its own right, yet it is embedded within a larger whole. Holonic systems tend to generate order from the bottom up for the mutual benefit of both the smaller, embedded systems and the larger, embracing systems. The larger systems go beyond the smaller ones, yet still include them and depend on them.

We can take this thinking as far as we wish and say that the world loves what we do to serve ourselves. Committing to our soul's agenda contributes to the agenda of a living world. Kindness to ourselves contributes to kindness in the world. The world evolves by our evolution.

Taking the point-of-view of the larger system, we see that when we make choices in harmony with natural systems, nature backs us up. We embody the cycles of life through our choices: we nurture new projects with parental care; we delight in them as they come to fruition; we let them go when their time passes. Or we set a boundary that operates like the cell's semi-permeable membrane. Or we get into a task and then gracefully disengage from it like the waves that roll in and roll out.

When we operate as nature operates, we take our place in the complex web of life. From that place our choices ripple out through the web to influence the whole system. We feel life flowing through us, and that's as satisfying as it gets.

PART III

CHANGE,
AND WHAT IT
BRINGS

CHAPTER 7

CHANGE

Change is mysterious. Sometimes it just happens and we're not quite sure how. Other times we try and try, and nothing works. More often than we think, the change that truly shifts things is more a gift than an act. It comes to us; we don't go to it. Although we may not be able to summon change, we can make a congenial environment for it to show up.

In this chapter, you'll encounter three change models—one of which you'll work with in more detail—so you can recognize change more readily when it comes. The model that you'll explore in the greatest depth uses so-called bad feelings to help point you in the direction of fundamental change. Throughout the process, you'll learn about allies, both internal and external, that you can call upon to lend their support. The chapter closes with special techniques that can come in handy along the way. Let's begin!

The Path—Ever Steady Progress to the Shining Goal Or...

Wouldn't it be nice if change took the form we would expect—a steady upward climb where results are directly commensurate with efforts? That's not how it usually goes. Instead the path is wayward. Change seems to loop back on itself. We get the same challenges again and again, so it's hard to know if we're making progress at all. Or we put in a lot of effort, nothing seems to happen, then, voilà! We change.

Punk Eke

For his model of evolutionary change, paleontologist Steven Jay Gould coined the term "punk-eke," short for "punctuated equilibrium." Things go along for awhile in a fairly steady state. Then, Something Happens and we find ourselves in a different place, perhaps without quite knowing how we got there. This model sees change as proceeding by quantum leaps—or maybe quantum baby-steps! The change is not steady, but happens in spurts. This model requires faith on the part of the person changing. We have to trust that our efforts will bear fruit, that eventually we'll pop through to a new level and find ourselves on the next rung of the ladder.

Progress and Integration

Another change model is progress and integration, effort and recovery, also known as "two steps forward, one step back." We boldly venture out to our leading edge, seriously stretching ourselves, and then come back to the center to integrate what we learned and replenish our resources. This is the way change happens for many people. It allows time for not-doing as well as doing.

This model also requires faith. In the "one step back" phase, we feel like we're backsliding—not doing it. We have to trust that we won't go all the way back to where we started. Instead, the turnaround spot moves a bit ahead each time. Think about it. If you weren't on the path, you wouldn't even recognize when you backslide. You'd have no forward motion to orient you. In this model, we acknowledge the step backward as part of the process and welcome it as much as the two steps forward.

What to Do While Waiting For Change to Show Up

In my first book, I told of how I dealt with the chronic migraine headaches that I was trying to relieve. As the headache came on I would go into "help-the-headache" mode. I'd do slow neck rolls, massage my temples, tense-and-release my shoulder muscles. I would lay off sardines, chocolate, and peanuts, the very foods I wanted to eat. I would shade my eyes, put in earplugs, and drink warm water. None of the things I did actually took away the migraine. They just made me more comfortable as I waited it out.

Acupuncture finally shifted my neural circuits, yet the "help-the-headache" routine became part of my post-migraine life and, no doubt, contributed to making future headaches less frequent.

As we wait for time management change to show up, there's much we can do. We can cultivate centered attention. We can establish firm and flexible boundaries. We can make our choices more consciously. Not only do these activities soothe that part of us that just wants to do *something*, they prepare the ground for the shift and actually address the distress.

Legend tells us that the real shift—the one that fundamentally changes everything—often appears very modestly. It doesn't come with trumpets and drums. Deep shifts appear when we are able to receive them. Sometimes the best thing we can do is keep our attention open and welcoming, practice the skills, and trust that the shift is on its way. This time the conditions may be right. This approach might click in. This time we might change deeply and forever.

Turning Bad Stuff into Good Stuff

If we learn how to use our mistakes as well as our accomplishments, everything we do—whether we feel it is "good" or "bad"—moves us along. The process of turning difficulties into lessons, changing so-called bad stuff into good stuff, is reminiscent of the old alchemist's art and science of turning lead into gold. We use our difficulties as the *prima materia,* the raw material, of time management change.

First, we establish a realistic starting point by telling the truth about our experience. Next, we use recurring difficult feelings from our experience as signposts leading to a leverage point where change will have the most effect. Lastly, at that leverage point we loosen the hold the bad stuff has on us. We turn our difficulties into guides pointing towards powerful change.

Throughout the change process it's useful to have help. We can summon aspects of ourselves as internal allies for support and perspective. Four allies walk with us along the path of change—the

Curious Anthropologist, the Bold Explorer, the Creative Artist, and the Compassionate Witness.

Curious Anthropologist

This ally's response to everything is, "That's interesting!" Every event, every thought, every feeling, every reaction, every consequence is fascinating. It's all relevant. This scientist welcomes all data, whether it fits into the hypothesis or not. In fact, things that don't fit are opportunities to expand, refine, and develop the hypothesis. The Curious Anthropologist helps us discover that challenges are not only interesting, but also relevant and valuable.

Bold Explorer

This ally is eager and able to do something new and venture into the unknown. The Bold Explorer has stamina to endure trials, tolerance for discomfort, and gumption to press on. This ally's catchphrase— "Let's go for it!"—really comes in handy when we try out new behaviors that feel uncomfortable.

Creative Artist

This ally generates unlimited possibilities. If there's a stumbling block, this innovator is at the ready with an intriguing solution, "What about this? Or this? Or this?" They love thinking "outside the box." Some of the Creative Artist's most improbable ideas turn into workable strategies.

Compassionate Witness

This ally holds everything in kindly awareness, utterly without judgment. It's all good and true. Guided by the heart and spirit, this nurturer has unfailing benevolence and acceptance of what is. The Compassionate Witness accompanies us through the entire change process and is especially helpful in the beginning.

Truth-Telling

People often jump into change as if they were diving into the deep end of a pool—eyes squeezed shut, holding their noses. By an act of will, they just jump off. When this works, it's mostly by plain luck. We serve ourselves better by keeping our eyes open, breathing, and looking before we leap. Then we might learn valuable lessons that make change all the more powerful. So the first step is to be aware.

It's all too easy to run on auto-pilot, oblivious to the truth of what's actually happening. We do it all the time. We wish we were other than what we are. We hope things will turn out as we envision them. We expect ourselves to be a certain way. But we need to tell the truth. In the Attention chapter you began to develop awareness and cultivate a steadier inner core of attention. That's the place to start.

Telling the truth about our experience takes the help of several internal allies. Our Curious Anthropologist looks at all the data—no editing, no judging. Among the data are the physical facts of the matter, the context and history, our uncomfortable feelings and unrealistic expectations, our not-always-pleasant responses, our resistance, mistakes and troublesome habits, and the consequences of our actions/reactions. We see the situation in all its complexity without the spin of criticism or judgment. Our Bold Explorer is willing to bear the discomfort of looking at all that bad stuff because the Bold Explorer knows there is a reward just around the corner. The Creative Artist sees that what's happening is just one option out of many that we could've chosen. Yet, since the option we did choose might be hard to bear, the Compassionate Witness stands steadfastly with us.

Scouting for Feeling-Habits

As we witness the truth of our experience, we invariably find a difficult feeling that surfaces again and again. For example, we notice that we're always critical of ourselves and everyone around us. Or we tend to habitually worry about the future. Or anger is never far away when things don't go fast enough. Or we're chronically anxious about looking bad before others. Or we're resigned to overwork. Or we bully ourselves into doing things we'd rather not.

These feeling-habits permeate our emotional life. For the most part, we're unaware of them, and if we do become aware of them, we often deny them. We try to put aside our anger, or not feel so despondent, or not worry so much. And if we can't do that, we invent scores of reasons and justifications for their existence.

In using bad feelings to help us change, there's little need to psychologize. It doesn't really matter how, when, or why we came to have these uncomfortable feelings. The fact is, we have them. In some real sense, these feelings flow completely reasonably from beliefs about ourselves and the world.

In the change process, the Compassionate Witness helps us bear the fact that we have these feelings. The Bold Explorer helps us track them down not to find their cause, or get rid of them, but to use them as the raw material for change.

The Leverage Point

When we identify this all too familiar feeling, we've found the leverage point, the crux of our distress, where applying effort will make a real difference. Think of it, changing a habit that comes up again and again changes everything! It's like stopping smoking or any addiction. The results are spectacular. And since the issue comes up constantly, we have plenty of opportunities to practice.

The effort required is, however, considerable. A feeling-habit is like a huge stone buried in hardened clay. It's not easy to move, much less see. Yet with a little work we can loosen the ground around it, and begin to dislodge it.

Applying Effort

You can call on all of these allies to work the leverage point, to get a crowbar in there and begin to free up the feeling-habit. Here are a few possible ways to apply effort, followed by three examples.

Raising awareness

The simple act of raising awareness is a good technique. You can step back from the feeling-habit and view it as the Curious Anthropologist, interested in everything, judging nothing. From this point of view you'll see a larger picture. Often, the mere act of becoming aware begins to loosen a feeling-habit's hold. When you step back and become aware, you put a little bit of space between yourself and the feeling-habit. As you raise your awareness, you become conversant with your particular view of reality. You get to know intimately the lens through which you see things. The Curious Anthropologist helps you see the feeling neutrally—it is just information.

The Compassionate Witness grants you the circumstances that brought you to the feeling-habit. There was, more than likely, a good reason for the feeling arising once upon a time. Now you can practice kindness and non-judgment of yourself and others, which plants the seed of acceptance. But acceptance doesn't mean endorsement; you still want to change.

Rewriting the script

The Creative Artist can help you play with the feeling-habit in ways that offer some wiggle-room. This imaginative play has the potential for expanding your hypothesis of how things are. Most of us believe the way it is, is The Way It Is. Yet the Creative Artist suggests that may not be so.

For instance, you could rewrite your script. Maybe you feel like you habitually cave into your friends' demands and end up saying "Yes!" all the time. You could try out a different scenario in your imagination. Imagine yourself saying "No," firmly, gently, and utterly. Although this scenario is certainly uncomfortable, play with it. If you do, you learn what comes up for you when you say "No." (Take a look back at the Choices chapter for an exploration of what we have to give up when we launch a new behavior.) The Bold Explorer can help you bear the unfamiliarity and discomfort as you give it a try.

The very act of imagining lays down tracks for the new behavior. It's said that what happens in our imaginations—and in our dreams—actually makes physical neural connections that allow behavior to change more easily. (This works both ways, of course, so we'd be wise to choose well what we imagine.)

Another technique is to brainstorm a complete resolution of the situation. Let your Creative Artist loose to invent numerous ways to resolve the issue. For example, take the scenario above when you're worried about always saying "Yes!" Imagine that you and a friend who wants you to do something you don't want to do agree to abide by the roll of dice. Or, imagine that a kindly, dispassionate, faithful sentry stops your friend at a boundary gate. The sentry respectfully brings the request to you, the King in the throne room, for your decision, and then shuttles back to your friend with the answer. You could imagine that you have "Asking Hours" when the "grantor-of-requests" is available. You could even imagine displaying your full plate of things to do to your friend and offering her the opportunity to give input on your priorities.

Each one of these fanciful ideas has a seed of a useful strategy. You may get better at saying "No" just by imagining doing so. You may put the decision in the hands of some mutually trusted neutral party. You may establish specific times for taking requests. You may find ways to be more collaborative in your decision-making process.

Taking action

The point, of course, is to take action, to do something different, to actually change. Truth-telling alone might give you information about the course of action to take—what changes to make, in what order, and what you might reasonably expect. For example, a client wanted to use a Tickler File reminder system, but it wasn't working for her. As she played out using the tickler in her imagination, she could see that she hadn't pulled apart the tasks of her project yet. Her reminders were too general, and they didn't really help her in day-to-day time management. In her eagerness to get on with it, she had skipped steps and gotten ahead of herself. Once she imagined actually using the tickler she could see what she needed to do to set up a system that worked.

On the verge of taking action, powerful resistance often shows up. It's a sign that the action we're about to take could make a real difference. The part of us that prefers things to be familiar, despite how ineffective or uncomfortable they are, puts on the brakes, hard. But we do want to change. Here's where the Bold Explorer comes in. We acknowledge our resistance, listen to it (it may have valuable information for us), and change anyway. (One definition of madness is to continue to do the same thing, yet expect a different result.)

Desire, willpower, and guilt

Wanting to change doesn't necessarily make us change. Even our strongest desires and intentions, useful as they are to align ourselves and clarify our goals, don't guarantee that change will happen. Heroic acts of willpower and strict discipline don't seem to work either. We may do what our will dictates for a while, but then we rebel against the taskmaster cracking the whip and mutiny! Guilt doesn't make us change either. The act of feeling bad soothes the part of us that's trying to do something, anything. So, we feel lousy—isn't that enough?

As it turns out, desire, willpower, and guilt rarely help us change. What does is presence—being able to bear the truth, seeing it from a wider perspective, and staying with it long enough to work with it. That prepares fertile ground for the seed of change to sprout.

Three Feeling-Habits

It's said that when we have an issue—with time management or, indeed, with anything—it's how we are with the issue that's the issue. If we learn to work with the feeling-habits that arise in the face of our time management issues, we've gone a long way towards resolving them. If, instead of denying the feelings, inventing justifications for them, or even putting them aside, we engage them directly, we are well on the way to change. Here are three feeling-habit stories, told in the first person, along with some ideas of how to work with them.

Irritated

I notice that I get irritated when my partner keeps me waiting. Then I get irritated in traffic, when a friend implies I did something that I didn't, when the weather is foul, and when a colleague interrupts me in the middle of writing. I notice myself getting irritated again, and again, and again. This feeling-habit, along with its fellows—anger, resentment, and impatience—is certainly a familiar visitor. Second-cousins to these feeling-habits, such as criticism of others, justification of my behavior, and blame of anybody or anything (myself included), often tag along with them.

Merely raising awareness begins to loosen things up. It's said that, "When you see the wolf, you see him everywhere." So, I continue to notice this feeling arising again and again in me. After a while I feel like the cartoon character Wile E. Coyote trying to trap the Road-runner again and again. It does get funny. However, I'm kind with myself as I'm amused.

I notice that my irritation involves an intense focus on whomever or whatever happens to be irritating me. I get pushy; my boundaries get spiky. I find that if I widen my focus, step back, and soften up a bit, things look (and feel) considerably different. I acknowledge that my partner is always late; that's just how he is. My friend doesn't have all the information; she's just making an assumption based on what she knows. The weather is the weather. To my colleague, his issue is the most important thing in the world. These are the facts of the matter. If I can acknowledge those facts, the irritation begins to subside.

Acknowledging the facts gives me information to make some changes—like changing my expectations of my partner and making sure my friend has all the information. Shifting my focus from the other person who's irritating me to myself helps too. I get centered within my own appropriately firm boundary so that when the colleague interrupts, I can stay with my own agenda.

Anxious

I notice that I get anxious when I'm nearing the end of a project and put on the brakes. Then I find myself anxious when I'm getting ready to leave the house. I'm anxious going into a meeting and stay anxious all the way through it. I know I'm anxious because I have difficulty catching a full breath. This feeling-habit, along with its siblings, fear, worry, and panic and its cousins, distraction, restlessness, and confusion, are familiar.

Paying attention to my thoughts in the midst of anxiety I find a lot of scattered "what-if" worries. What would I do next if I finish the project? What's going to happen when I go out? Will I be prepared enough in the meeting? Will I get an opportunity to talk? These worries mostly go nowhere and just compromise attention to the task at hand.

In order to actively engage with what's before me, I need to soothe the anxiety, so I call in the Creative Artist to come up with ideas of what to do. Sometimes all I need is to talk the issue through with a friend. Sometimes going for a brisk walk will do the trick. Most often, however, I need to take some form of action. I'm anxious because there's something I need to do that I'm not doing.

The Curious Anthropologist helps me identify what I can do. I can make a plan for when I finish the project—that will help. Or I can prepare for the meeting—that will help, too. Whatever action I take I do within the contained, protected space of a task boundary; I use the three-phase close-down—this also helps. I don't get overwhelmed, yet I log in actual time doing the task I'm anxious about.

I call on the Compassionate Witness to hold my hand as I venture, vulnerable, into the unpredictable world out there. The Witness reassures me that there will be mistakes, and that's OK. The Bold Explorer comes along to help me step into the abyss with my eyes wide open. It will be uncomfortable, but that's OK too. Accompanied by all my allies I can attend to the task at hand, do what needs doing, and soothe my anxiety.

Discouraged

I notice that I get discouraged when my To Do list is much too long and I'm doing only a fraction of what I should or am capable of. I get discouraged when I'm just going through the motions with the tasks I do manage to get done. Things take a lot longer than I think they should. I can't seem to make a decision or priority call. This feeling-habit, along with its fellows—resignation, despair, hopelessness, and negativity—drag me down.

Raising awareness by monitoring my energy clues me into the feeling-habit since it often comes with waves of fatigue that wash over me out of nowhere. Aware of my low energy, I might simply get more rest, do some enlivening exercise, or take better care of myself. However, there might be a lot more to it than that. I track the feeling back a bit and see that getting more sleep only touches the surface of the issue.

My Curious Anthropologist observes a lot of "shoulds" and calls in the Creative Artist to help. So, says the Artist, how about imagining the worst that could happen? (Yikes, I say—get some support from the Bold Explorer, now!) I play out a few imaginary scenarios. For example, I do only what I can, not what I think I should, and it's about half of what I expect. I let things take as long as they take, and they eat up my whole day. I allow the priorities to fall where they may, and those who have a stake in them get upset. I don't go through the motions, and tasks fall through the cracks.

As I play out each scene, I notice that not only are some of my worst fears not so bad, but I can actually do something about them. I can negotiate with those who have a stake in what I do. I can use the three-phase close-down to contain tasks that take a long time. Most importantly, I can release unrealistic expectations.

The Anthropologist also notices that the spark is gone and there's no sense of satisfaction with what I do. The Creative Artist can help here too. I put aside the To Do list, which seems to have no "Ooooh, I *want* to do that!" items on it, and go for a walk to Main Street or the mall to see what catches my eye. Which display attracts me? Which colors do I like? What textures and materials beckon? As I return, I keep my feelers out for attractive things along the way—the rustle of leaves, a lively dog, the scent of blossoms. Then, with list in hand, I scan it to find even a shred of "Ooooh!" and do that task. The next step is crucial. I allow myself to feel the satisfaction of doing something attractive on my list.

As I step back from my habitual focus of falling short and find more "Ooooh!", life looks considerably different. With the Bold Explorer leading me on, the Curious Anthropologist sniffing out the facts, the Creative Artist coming up with fanciful yet helpful scenarios, and the Compassionate Witness holding my hand (because, indeed, there are not-so-nice things going on), I see there is plenty to be deeply and legitimately grateful for. The sky is blue, I got out of bed, and someone completely unknown to me gave me a smile. Gratitude dissolves my discouragement. I give thanks.

You may have a feeling-habit similar to those described above, yet the way it plays out in your life and how you work with it may be very different. Anger, fear, sadness, and all the other human feelings have particular nuances in each particular life. Look to the Resource section for more ideas about feeling-habits and how to work with them.

The Results—Acceptance, Tolerance for Good Feelings, Kindness to Ourselves

As we work this model, we find that not only can we survive bad feelings, these feelings give us opportunities to work the leverage point. We don't have to obsess about our difficulties or avoid them.

We can welcome bad feelings as well as good, since they give us useful information.

Acceptance of our entire reality—the so-called good and the so-called bad—opens us to acceptance of others and of life on earth. We must remember that acceptance doesn't mean endorsement. We still want to grow towards something better. But we can walk the path of change with equanimity, eagerly scouting for the next challenge.

As we change, we need to build up our capacity to experience the unfamiliar feelings of comfort, happiness, forgiveness, and calm. Conversely, we let go of attachment to drama, discomfort, angst, and alienation. This is a lot harder than it sounds. Difficult feelings, for all their negativity, have a lot of charge. When we're in the midst of them, we can't help but feel alive—it hurts so much. As we change, however, we get good at letting positive feelings sink in, blossom, and bear fruit. We feel the satisfaction and power of taking our lives into our own hands.

We also need to grant ourselves some slack. When the big crunch comes, and our resolve to leave work on time caves in, we're flexible enough to stay late this once and comp out the time. When we find ourselves frittering away time on minor matters, we take a real break rather than crack the whip. When our list suddenly overwhelms us, we step back and make some decisions. It's not that we're bad, lazy, or spineless. Circumstances around us may have changed or what we thought would work no longer does. The Compassionate Witness can help us be kind to ourselves.

Helpful Techniques

Several techniques you've encountered in other guises earlier in the book are particularly useful as we change.

Gaining Traction

A big challenge in the change process is to feel like we're getting somewhere, especially at the beginning. Although we wish the fairy godmother would change us instantaneously with her magic wand, it usually doesn't happen like that. Instead, the process is gradual, and especially slow at the beginning. For instance, we might notice just a little change in attitude when we don't beat ourselves up so much as we procrastinate.

Paying attention to any progress, however small, gathers evidence that things are changing. The more we do it, the better we become at recognizing progress. The body of evidence grows, like a snowball gathering weight as it rolls downhill, or an indistinct hologram becoming clearer as more information accumulates. By shifting our attention from what we're doing wrong to what we're doing right, we begin to feel like we're making progress.

The step of rewriting the script may also provide evidence on our behalf. For example, we take a wider view of our procrastinating habit and see that indeed, we need time to sit with the project and just do nothing. Knowing this, we include doing-nothing time, as well as task time, into our plan.

The Reset Button

When we find ourselves sliding down a slippery slope, continuing to do something that's not serving us, we need to push the Reset Button to break up the behavior that's getting us into trouble. We pause, step out of the action, feeling, or thought, and step back in, but differently. A few techniques that focus on the physical can help you do so.

One technique is to widen your visual field to take in more of the scene. The change of focus puts what you're doing into a broader context where the difficult behavior may not be so compelling. Another technique is to take a few conscious breaths to center yourself in your body and slow yourself down. Or you can take a walk, do some physical exercise, or just change your body position. You can notice something interesting in the person you're with or the environment—a color in their clothes, the shape of their eyebrow, the light coming in a window. Noticing something positive or even neutral reminds us that even in a situation that's uncomfortable, both "good" and "bad" coexist. All of these techniques help us stop the pattern, get back to neutral gear, and reorient ourselves.

External Allies

Beyond our cast of internal helpers, we have external allies to call upon for support. There's nothing quite like being witnessed by people who are dear to us and to whom we are dear. Our good buddies are eager to help, even though we think they don't have time for us. In some sense it may be true—who has time for anyone these days? However, when we ask for help we give others leave to ask in return. We offer them the opportunity to feel good by helping us. Thus we feed our mutual interconnection. We can also seek help from professionals of all sorts—coaches, counselors, therapists, readers, and advisors. When we enlist others in our change process we feel held in the web of life.

Change Is What Life Is All About

The change process is difficult and scary. Couldn't things just remain the same forever, as they do in some versions of heaven? But that's not how it goes here on earth. Change is what life is about—growth, transformation, evolution. Rabbi Gershon Winkler in his article, *Welcome to the Garden of Paradox* says, "In the spirit world you cannot execute the actual becoming, the infinite possibilities of transformation with which you are endowed. This only happens here, in this world, in the world of change, in the realm of instability, in the cauldron of relativity, in the arena of opportunity, the gauntlet of challenge."[14]

To participate fully in this grand enterprise of life on earth takes flexibility, courage, and compassion. We try something new; we take a chance; we forgive our past and let it go. As we walk into our lives, we translate our changing desires into changing reality. Our lives are at every moment something completely new. What an adventure!

CHAPTER 8

THE FRUITS OF THE PRACTICE

The new time management develops three capacities. Vitality is the felt sense of being alive, of participating in the grand enterprise of life on earth. Creativity is the ability to express ourselves using whatever materials are at hand. Discernment is the faculty of seeing things clearly and making distinctions amongst them. These capacities, or virtues if you will, make us ever more fully human, more of who we are meant to be. The new time management also contributes to your evolution and that of the world.

Vitality

What we say we want from time management is to do what we have to do in the time available, to not be so overwhelmed, to deal effectively with competing demands. But what we really seek, deep down, is the sense that we're truly living our lives, not just working through a To Do list. When we get to the end of life, we want to know with certainty that we have lived.

Feeling Alive Only When...

In activity-oriented America, being alive seems to be about doing lots of things. We drive while talking on the phone while plugged into an iPod while eating lunch while keeping an ear out for a message alert while navigating via GPS on the in-vehicle screen. This is not uncommon. The more we do the more alive we seem to be.

If we can't do a lot, at least what we do can be exciting. We take up high-energy/high-risk sports. We, along with popular broadcast media personalities, speak quickly and loudly. We interrupt each other and rarely take time to listen. Our media experiences are often violent, suspense-ridden, and filled with high drama in fast cuts. Our hearts are beating loudly; we must be alive.

We focus on anything but the present. Hiking up a mountain we think, "Won't it be great to get a real view!" Then, after hours of struggle, we finally make the summit. The view spreads out before us; we look ... and then we leave. That's it. We're unpracticed in letting the moment reverberate, in taking in the experience.

Our heavily mediated, commercialized environment, which relies on our dissatisfaction for its productivity engine, has, in a very real sense, deadened us to life itself. Whatever we have, more would be better. We're always waiting for the exciting moment when things are really real. What we do or have in the present is but a pale, thin version of the wonderful things we could do or have in the future. So we never quite feel alive.

Feeling Alive, Period

The key to cultivating vitality, the felt experience of life, is the simple cliché, Be Here Now. It centers on Attention. As we attend more fully, we find, as Eckhart Tolle says, "a genuine sense of aliveness."[15] We become one with life.

As we practice attention to our experience, we find the vitality inherent in all of it. What's happening right here, right now is deep, rich, and nuanced, even though the commercial culture might pooh-pooh it as not exciting, productive, or future-oriented. In our simple, still presence we are intensely alive.

We no longer wait for future satisfaction; we find it now, in every moment. The drama and angst of the media stories are less compelling; we feel a stronger pull to be simply who we are. Negativity is not our default mode; we see all sides of the situation. When we attend to our felt experience, vitality is no longer conditional. It is available to us always. We expand our capacity for satisfaction, joy, and peace, we feel alive. Period.

The Way in Life

At the beginning of Part II—the ABCs, you encountered the Brotherhood of the Common Life, a Christian monastic order in the fourteenth century where members did not withdraw into cloisters but rather practiced the "way in life." They participated in secular life without being in thrall to it. They maintained the perspective from the bank of the river of experience without being swept away in the flow. Our time management practice offers this perspective—we step into the river and out of it when needed. With access to both the view from the shore and the experience of the river, we embrace the whole of life.

Creativity

A basic human function is to create. In the Judeo-Christian tradition, we are made in the image of the Divine whose primary function is Creator. We are, by nature, creative. Practicing time management as a creative project offers an ever-available, ever-renewable source of raw material—the moments of our lives. We shape them as the potter molds clay or the sculptor works marble and, in so doing, create a life which is a work of art.

We handle our moments as artists, picking and choosing, forming and shaping, so our lives are an outward expression of who we truly are. (Hopefully, the likeness is a good one!) Time management as creative artwork calls forth our awareness on all levels. Everything—the smallest details, the grandest pattern, and everything in between—is material. It's all useful and relevant to the work at hand.

Since the only things we really "own" are the moments of our lives, they are the only gifts we can truly give. Through our creative choices, we make unique connections that only we can make. We reconcile rifts between values deep within us and those we see around us. Our lives contribute to the great artwork unfolding around and through us.

Expression

Expressing ourselves is a particularly human thing to do and, with time management, there's no way to avoid it. Every choice (or non-choice) we make expresses who we are. Our rushing about shows that we value speed. Our worry about the future shows that we might not trust life fully. How we deal with an interruption shows how we respect ourselves, our tasks, and other people. Our time management choices express our values, what makes sense to us, what our place in society is, and how we are embedded in nature. When we choose with both our inner desires and the outer environment in all its complexity in mind, the artwork we create is certainly grand!

Integritas, Consonantia, Claritas

St. Thomas Aquinas identified three qualities of beauty—*integritas*, *consonantia*, and *claritas*.[16] *Integritas* is the quality of wholeness. Our lives are of a piece. We operate from a steady center and stay true to ourselves with integrity. *Consonantia* is the quality of harmony. Even though our lives have many parts, each part relates to the others. For example, at work we remember an exchange with our child that enlivens our project. A conversation with a colleague gives us an idea for our hobby. Exercise at the gym builds community.

As we embody *integritas* and *consonantia*, *claritas*, is born. *Claritas* is the quality of radiance, shining forth like light from a star. *Claritas* propels us into the world with dynamic, fruitful engagement. Through *claritas* we exercise loving, compassionate power.

A Musical Example

The performing arts in particular—music, dance, and drama—offer models for using the moments of our days as raw material for artwork. Here is an example from classical music. A composer creates a moving pattern of sound by playing with texture, timing, and tension. The pattern unfolds, transforms, repeats, and eventually sinks back into silence. The challenge is to create a beautiful piece. The composer's art is to make the piece hang together, to reconcile the dilemmas and difficulties. Though it may not answer all the questions it raises, nor be sweet or "pretty," it points towards truth—and that is powerfully satisfying.

Time management as creative practice makes sense out of what we do day by day, moment by moment, so that it hangs together and rings true. We listen to the inner voice and, at the same time, respond to what's before us in the outer world. We engage not only our choosing will, but also our sense of play and intuition. The dynamic interaction between our deepest selves and the circumstances of which we are a part brings our way of being out into the world for all to see. Thus we play our particular part in the great symphony of life.

Discernment

Discernment is the human capacity to say "No" as well as "Yes." It's the capacity to draw a line and place some things on this side and others on that side. Discernment is related to capacities like discrimination, criticism, propriety, and judgment. How loaded these words seem! Discrimination brings to mind negative preferential treatment—as in job discrimination. Criticism seems to be about making negative statements regarding bad behavior. Propriety seems stuffy and, well, inappropriate in our informal, casual environment. And, of course, judgment is something we avoid whenever possible.

Yet we need these very capacities to make choices that serve ourselves, others, and the greater good. We need to discriminate—to make fine distinctions. We need to exercise our critical abilities—to see what works and what doesn't. We need to do things in a proper manner, appropriate to the task. We need to use good judgment—weighing all the factors impartially. These capacities all contribute to discernment.

We often balk at judgment and criticism because we overuse them; they make up so much of our internal chatter. We walk through life thinking "They're not as slim as I am," or "Look at those wonderful shoes; mine are shameful." We continually make comparisons and put ourselves one up or one down. The trick is to use judgment judiciously!

Discernment comes from listening to not just the thinking, judging mind, but also the feeling body and heart which gives us a more realistic picture about what's actually happening. Here is a scenario. Today I had a whole list of catch-up tasks to do. I worked at them well for a good while, and then my body started to balk. I became restless and slightly headachy. My feelings gave a dip. I felt a bit discouraged, put upon, obligated. Paying attention to the signals from my body and heart, I decided to close down what I was doing and take a walk. Upon my return I realized I had done enough catch-up for the day. I'd do more tomorrow, but for today—done!

Letting Go

In traditional Chinese thought, discernment is associated with the element Metal whose time of year is autumn when the leaves fall. One November morning, I woke with a dream image—a dumpster with the company name emblazoned on it—Kristan. My dreamer showed me just how much there was to release, like the thousands of leaves blowing from the trees. I needed to draw my metal sword and decide what to do and what not to do; what to keep, what to throw away; what of my personal baggage from the past I'd outgrown and what was enduring and valuable.

To make these decisions we take up a position slightly distanced from the issue at hand where we see differences clearly, without giving a negative spin to what we see. We exercise the critical faculty without criticism, we judge without punishment, we discern without prejudicial discrimination. We draw the line and let what's on the "No" side go.

Hozho, the tightrope walker, and Goldilocks

In Navajo tradition, the fundamental state to be cultivated is *hozho*, the Beauty Way. For the Navajo, beauty is not so much pleasing and pretty, but balanced and proper. The word "proper" sounds old-fashioned but, in fact, propriety is the key to discernment—doing what's appropriate at the appropriate time.

Living appropriately is, in the Navajo way, what we humans are meant to do. It's evident in our bodies. With our feet on the ground and our heads reaching toward the stars, we are the bridge between earth and sky. Yes, we are like the spirits in heaven, and yes, we are like the animals on earth. Our greatest challenge is to maintain the delicate balance between these two natures. We honor both the animal conditions of time, space, feelings, and body and the spiritual conditions of free will, aspiration, the complex of obligations we've accepted, and our agenda for this life.

The word *balance* might suggest some serene state, unaffected by the buffeting forces swirling by, but consider the tightrope walker on the high wire. Although she appears calm, she is constantly responding to vectors both internal and external to maintain that balance. Balance is dynamic and, in fact, worth a standing ovation!

Goldilocks's encounter with the Three Bears (not too hot, not too cold, but just right) points us towards the balance point. The pace of life isn't too fast or too slow. We don't worry about the future, yet we make appropriate plans. We don't regret the past, yet we learn from experience. We base expectations on a proper mix of outer obligations and inner desires. We honor both our individuality and our place in the web of connections. As we do so, we participate in the ever-changing dance of life.

Evolution

The point of time management practice is to grow, to change, and to evolve. As you saw in the chapter on Change, this is what life on earth is all about. By managing time, you contribute to your own individual evolution and to that of the larger entities of which you are a part.

Personal Evolution

Through time management, you become more fully who you really are. You take the unique place in the web of life that is yours by birthright. Stepping into that place, you find deep satisfaction in being the person you are. You act as a sovereign being who can exercise power in service to the whole.

Satisfaction

Satisfaction practice, encountered first in the Attention chapter, counterbalances habitual negative focus. Satisfaction is available at every turn. You may not have a concrete product to show, but you let the satisfaction of what you did reverberate (even if all you did was show up). Even when life is unpleasant or unfruitful, you acknowledge "bad" things as fuel for the enterprise. Nothing is wasted, everything is useful. You embrace your whole self and rest in the deep satisfaction that comes from unconditional acceptance.

Sovereignty

In *Steering By Starlight,* Martha Beck says that, "Freedom is available at any time, to anyone—and so is captivity."[17] Practicing the new time management you see that you need not be prey to every passing fancy. A steady core of attention centers you, and appropriate boundaries protect you; you make choices as a free agent. You find that you feel less enslaved to such things as regret for the past, worry for the future, habits of mind or feeling, or external demands. You get in touch with your own agenda, needs, desires, and life purpose. Sovereignty calls forth your power to influence the world.

Service

You exercise that power to serve the greater good of all in every choice you make. Each choice, even those that seem to serve just you, contributes to making a better world. You know in your bones that you are included when you speak of "the greater good of all." With this is mind, you serve gladly, unreservedly, since whatever you do is for the mutual benefit of yourself and the world. As your sovereignty grows, so does your service. As we are free, so may we be bound.

A grand project

Managing time offers a rare opportunity to do a "big number." It's a grand enterprise, like setting out on a long ocean voyage, building a homestead on the prairie, or creating artwork for a one-man show. Exercising attention, establishing good boundaries, making wise choices—these all call for sustained effort over the course of time.

Within the purview of the grand project, everything can and will come up—all our fears and anxieties, all our triumphs and frustrations, all our hopes and despair. Big projects have the capacity to enfold our whole being.

The Greater Evolution

When intense time pressure permeates the atmosphere we breathe, it's all too easy to accept it as a given, like the invisible air. Our charge, however, is to put something else into the mix. Attention, good boundaries, and conscious choices contribute to relieving the pressure and providing a more sustainable alternative.

Because we are engaged with the surrounding atmosphere whether we know it or not, whether we like it or not, the shift will follow naturally from our practice. That's good to know, especially if it feels uncomfortable to do something different from the norm.

The message of many spiritual and scientific figures and systems these days—from the Dalai Lama to Oprah Winfrey to theoretical physics—is that we are all one. What we do affects everything around us because, in fact, we *are* everything around us; separation is merely an illusion. What we do has great influence.

Nature backs you up, and vice versa

In the Choices chapter, you saw that the more we align ourselves with how natural systems operate, the more satisfying our time management choices can be. We both extend ourselves and replenish ourselves. We nurture projects through their life cycles. We let some things in and keep other things out. Our lives, in the small, mirror life in the large.

When we are so held by life, we may notice more easily what life brings to us. For example, we dream of a lively marketplace and so decide to enliven our interchanges with friends. We look up at the full moon and remember that our project is at its peak and we'll need to wind it down soon. We encounter a colleague who we haven't seen in a while and rekindle attention to the project we worked on together years ago. Messages are all around us, although it may take the curiosity, creativity, courage, and compassion of our internal allies to help us discern their meaning.

Laying down tracks

Those of us who take the first step on the path are brave and often alone. Taking a realistic time management stand can seem dangerous. We fear that we'll lose our job, our friends, our community. Yet, when we take a step, we encourage others to do the same. Someone at the office finally says "No" instead of automatically saying "Yes," and everyone heaves a sigh of relief—they now have permission to say "No," too.

The path of change is indistinct at first, especially if we're the lone trailblazer. Yet, as we walk, we begin to notice others with us on this route different from the well-traveled superhighways of modern American culture. We are all like mammals traveling in the underbrush amongst the dinosaurs. Acknowledging and supporting each other, we lay down tracks for others to follow. As many pass this way, a road comes into being.

REFERENCES

1 *The Compact Edition of the Oxford English Dictionary, Volume 1* (New York: Oxford University Press, 1984), 1711.

2 Richard Saul Wurman, *Information Anxiety* (New York : Doubleday, 1989).

3 Barry Schwartz, *The Paradox of Choice:Why More is Less.* (New York: Harper Perennial, 2004), 1–6.

4 Jacob Needleman, *Money and the Meaning of Life.* (New York: Currency Doubleday, 1991), 299–309.

5 *The American Heritage Dictionary of the English Language.* (Boston: Houghton Mifflin Company, 1969), 85. Attention is the "concentration of the mental powers upon an object; a close or careful observing or listening." The word has its roots in the concept of stretching giving us extension—stretching out to the full length, and intention—the aim towards which we stretch.

6 Woody Allen was purported to say, "90% of life is just showing up."

7 Martha Beck, *Finding Your Own North Star: Claiming the Life You Were Meant to Live* (New York: Crown Publishers, 2001), 59–79.

8 Rhonda Byrne, *The Secret* (New York: Atria Books, 2006).

9 Parker Palmer, interview by Bill Moyers, *Bill Moyers Journal,* PBS, February 20, 2009.

10 Barry Schwartz, *The Paradox of Choice:Why More is Less* (New York: Harper Perennial, 2004), 221.

11 Viktor E. Frankl, *Man's Search for Meaning* (New York: Washington Square Press, 1985), 21–115.

12 Stephen Harrod Buhner, *The Secret Teachings of Plants: The Intelligence of the Heart in the Direct Perception of Nature* (Rochester, VT: Bear & Company, 2004), 275–289.

13 Kurt Leland, *Menus for Impulsive Living: A Revolutionary Approach to Organizing and Energizing Your Life* (New York: Doubleday, 1989).

14 Winkler, Rabbi Gershon, "A Sojourn in the Garden of Paradox" (*The Center Post*, Fall 2009), 6.

[15] Eckhart Tolle, *A New Earth: Awakening to Your Life's Purpose* (New York: Penguin Group, 2005), 249.

[16] As expounded by Stephen Dedalus in James Joyce, *A Portrait of the Artist as a Young Man* (Everyman's Library, New York: Random House, 1991), 265.

[17] Martha Beck, *Steering By Starlight: Find Your Right Life No Matter What* (New York: Rodale Inc., 2008), 47

PART IV

RESOURCES

FURTHER READING

Abram, David. *The Spell of the Sensuous: Perception and Language in a More-than-human World.* New York: Pantheon Books, 1996.

Beck, Martha. *Finding Your Own North Star: Claiming the Life You Were Meant to Live.* New York: Crown Publishers, 2001.

_____. *Steering By Starlight: Find Your Right Life No Matter What.* New York: Rodale Inc., 2008.

Beesing, Maria, O.P., Robert J. Nogosek, C.S.C., and Patrick H. O'Leary, S.J. *The Enneagram: A Journey of Self Discovery.* Denville, NJ: Dimension Books, 1984.

Buhner, Stephen Harrod. *The Secret Teachings of Plants: The Intelligence of the Heart in the Direct Perception of Nature.* Rochester, VT: Bear & Company, 2004.

Byrne, Rhonda. *The Secret.* New York: Atria Books, 2006.

Frankl, Viktor E. *Man's Search for Meaning.* New York: Washington Square Press, 1985.

Goleman, Daniel. *Emotional intelligence.* New York: Bantam Books, 1995.

Judith, Anodea. *Wheels of Life: A User's Guide to the Chakra System,* St. Paul: Llewellyn Publications, 1987.

Kornfield, Jack. *A Path with Heart: A Guide through the Perils and Promises of Spiritual Life.* New York: Bantam Books, 1993.

Leland, Kurt. *Menus for Impulsive Living: A Revolutionary Approach to Organizing and Energizing Your Life.* New York: Doubleday, 1989.

Macy, Joanna. *Coming Back to Life: Practices to Reconnect Our Lives, Our World.* Stony Creek, CT: New Society Publishers, 1998.

McLaren, Karla. *Emotional Genius: Discovering the Deepest Language of the Soul.* Columbia, CA: Laughing Tree Press, 2001.

Needleman, Jacob. *Money and the Meaning of Life.* New York: Currency Doubleday, 1991.

_____ *Time and the Soul: Where Has All the Meaningful Time Gone—and Can We Get It Back?* New York: Currency/Doubleday, 1998.

Palmer, Parker. *Let Your Life Speak: Listening for the Voice of Vocation.* San Francisco: Jossey- Bass, 2000.

Schaef, Anne Wilson. *When Society Becomes an Addict.* San Francisco: Harper & Row, 1987.

Schwartz, Barry. *The Paradox of Choice: Why More is Less.* New York: Harper Perennial, 2004.

Tolle, Eckhart. *A New Earth: Awakening to Your Life's Purpose.* New York: Penguin Group, 2005.

Twyman, James. *The Moses Code: The Most Powerful Manifestation Tool in the History of the World.* Carlsbad, CA: Hay House, 2008.

Vitale, Joe. *The Attractor Factor: 5 Easy Steps for Creating Wealth (or Anything Else) from the Inside Out.* Hoboken, NJ: J. Wiley, 2005.

Winkler, Rabbi Gershon. "A Sojourn in the Garden of Paradox." *The Center Post,* Fall 2009.

Woods, Walt. *Letter to Robin: A Mini-Course in Pendulum Dowsing.* www.lettertorobin.org.

Wurman, Richard Saul. *Information Anxiety.* New York: Doubleday, 1989.

USEFUL PRACTICES

Here are time management practices arranged alphabetically within the ABC categories. Give yourself a few weeks to integrate the practice into your routine. Remember, too, that not every technique suits your situation, nor is every tool useful for you.

Attention Practices

Active or Archive Desktop Organization: Arrange your desktop so that all of the materials you use frequently are close at hand and those you use less often are further away. Instead of making horizontal piles, use a vertical sorter so you don't bury your papers.

Both / And Heartbeat Challenge: This group exercise identifies your particular difficulty with staying in touch with yourself while paying attention to others; it gives you ideas that could help. Assemble a group of at least five people. Have someone prompt participants through the exercise with several moments between each prompt. Each step is more difficult than the last. The prompts are: "Close your eyes and find your pulse ... Make a sound with your voice in time with your heartbeat ... While making your sound, open your eyes ... Make your sound louder, allowing those around you to hear it ... Listen to someone else's sound while making your own sound." Then process the exercise by writing down the point where you had trouble staying in touch with your heartbeat. Think of what would have made it easier for you to stay with it. Then think of the exercise in terms of "my agenda" rather than "my heartbeat." Brainstorm what would make it easier for you to stay with your agenda while paying attention to others' agendas.

CDR: Catch thoughts that run through your mind using such tools as a sticky, steno pad, desk calendar, 3x5 card, little notebook, e-mail, voice mail, or electronic device. Distribute it to where it will make the most sense to review it later. For example, a note for picking up dry cleaning can go in your purse; a note about a specific work project can go in that project's folder. Then, review it. Remember, review does not mean *do*. When all the ideas are together you can more easily decide what to do and what not to do.

Dog Commands: Train your attention like a kind yet firm master. "Stay" keeps your attention where it is, rather than having it slip off to a distraction. "Leave It" brings your attention back when you've either gotten off track or are hanging on to a thought or action long past its usefulness. "Come" or "Heel" help bring your attention back when you find you're not doing the task you said you'd do. "Down" helps when you jump levels—you either get into too much detail or get stuck on the broad, overview level.

Eagle / Ant View: The Eagle surveys the whole scene from above; the Ant is on the ground doing the work. The Ant can't see the big picture and the Eagle can't do the work. It's best to alternate between Eagle view and Ant view.

Jumping Around As A Strategy: Set up a multi-tasking arena where you keep several tasks open at the same time. Contain the time by setting a timer (see three-phase close-down). Allow more than the usual time to close down. Within the arena, circulate freely amongst the tasks, doing whatever presents itself. When the timer goes off, close down each task, one by one, making sure to identify the next step if it's not finished. If, while you're circulating, you get ideas for other tasks, either catch them (see CDR) or decide then and there to work on them. A good close-down is the key to multi-tasking.

Modes of Attention: Use the most appropriate mode for the task at hand. Loosen up habitual patterns by trying out a mode different from your usual.

Body/mind/heart/spirit: When something compromises your attention, check that each of the four aspects of your being is on board. Your body may want some movement; your mind might be racing; your heart may not be in it; your spirit may be languishing. Give that aspect some of what it needs. When you align all the aspects, attention flows more smoothly.

Depth/surface: Operate at a level appropriate to the task. When doing relatively simple tasks, skim the surface. When doing something new or involved, immerse yourself. Beware of habitually operating at either level. If all you do is skim the surface, you lose the richness and complexity that depth offers. If all you do is immerse yourself, you have trouble coming up for air to re-strategize and switch tasks if necessary.

Drama/calm: Pay attention to calm things—slow music, a bubbling fountain, gently rustling leaves, quiet speech—as much as dramatic things—exciting movies, fast driving, and intense arguments. If you only pay attention when the volume is turned up, that's all you'll notice. Open your attention to the richness and interest in both the calm and the dramatic.

Fast/slow: Be aware of your pace. If you're going too fast, do something that moves more slowly, like gardening, fishing, or croquet. If you're dragging, listen to up-tempo music, take a brisk walk, or play with a dog. Entrain to an activity at your desired pace.

Negative/positive: Focus on the negative when you're embarking on a risky venture. Envisioning the worst offers creative options and builds hardiness so you don't collapse when things don't go as planned. Focus on the positive as your usual mode. Life looks a lot better that way.

Present/future/past: Being present, here and now, is where you want to be most of the time. However, when you're doing something new, focus on the future so you can envision the steps to take. When a task is finished, focus on the past so you can learn from it. However, don't get caught up in worry about the future or regret for the past.

Toward / away from: Identify the direction from which the impetus for your action comes. Does a particular goal attract you? Are you leaning into it? Are you pushing a task away? Are you backing off from it? Are you shoving off from what you just did to propel you onward? Are you barreling through an obstacle? All of these are useful strategies; use whatever is appropriate. If you get stuck in certain patterns, try something different.

Pause Button: When you're in the middle of a task and something interrupts you—a phone call, an e-mail, a drop-in—press your internal "Pause" button to freeze your action. Jot down a trigger word or fix a visual image in your mind. Take the interruption. Come back to the trigger word or image to get back to where you were. Press "Play" to pick up exactly where you left off

Reality Check: Getting a bead on how long things actually take settles down anxiety and grounds you in reality. A reality check can happen on many levels, from merely noticing the clock as you enter and leave a task to doing a full-blown time / task analysis where you write down what you're doing at 15-minute intervals throughout the course of a day. Establish a range of data for tasks that take longer than you think they should—how long does it take on a normal day, on a leisurely day, and on a bare-bones minimum day. Remember, this is not how long you wish it would take, but how long it actually takes. Cut yourself some slack and cheerfully acknowledge the reality of the situation.

Satisfaction Practice: Shifting your focus to what you've done from what you need to do gives your accomplishments weight. Every time you let what you've done sink in, you become more energized and encouraged. You get better at recognizing progress. Everything you do has value.

"Sticky" Project Management: First, brainstorm tasks, making a sticky for each task component. Have them all at a similar level of detail—

not too general, not too specific. Next, write the time needed for each task on the sticky—the total elapsed time from when the task begins to when you finish it. Factor in time for people to get back to you, interruptions, and other demands, not just actual task-time. Note other resources needed as well, like special information needed, sign-offs, consultations, and buy-in. Account for these factors in the time needed as well. Then, lay out the project. Arrange the stickies one after another when the output of one task is the input of the next, or in a group when tasks occur within the same time frame. Then, add up the total elapsed time of the entire project. For tasks happening at the same time, use the time of the task that takes the longest. Work backwards from the deadline to determine the start date. If the result is not within the schedule, make adjustments. Lastly, incorporate the tasks into your reminder system. Keep the overall project layout for reference.

Tickler File: Make a set of 17 file folders—one for each month (January–December) and one for each week (1st, 2nd, 3rd, 4th, 5th). Whenever a task comes to you, put a reminder into the appropriate folder, tickling when you need to start in order to deliver on time. On the first of the month, open that month's folder and distribute the tickles into the week folders. On the first day of the week, open that week's folder and group the tickles by day, clipping each day's reminders together. Stage them in a vertical file on your desk. Each day, work through that day's tickles. Distribute whatever you have left to another day. If an undone tickle keeps showing up, decide whether to do it or not. Use the same reminder to tickle recurring tasks, moving it to the next occurrence when you've done it. A tickler can be electronic as well as physical. Enter tickles as above and access them as the weeks and months come up. With electronic ticklers, park the actual papers in a handy physical file, arranged chronologically.

To Do List: A list puts your plans on paper—or in an electronic medium—so you don't have to hold them in your head. Daily lists are ephemeral, thrown away before making a new one. You can update lists that continue for more than a day or two by boldly crossing out Done items and highlighting Yet To Do items. Draw a horizontal line across the middle of the page; put Maybes below the line and Musts above the line. If you use task categories like Body & Soul/Work & Play/Cycles & Surprises (see below under Choices), group items according to the categories. A list keeps your attention where it needs to be, soothes an anxious mind, and helps you identify what you need.

Boundary Practices

Clear Zone: Establish a clear zone—a time without interrupting walk-ins, phone calls, voice mails, or e-mails. To decide when to have your clear zone, notice when you receive the least interruptions; do it then. The time need not be long—twenty minutes is a start. Communicate your plan to those who would want your attention and be sure to let them know when you *will be* available. Once you've established a clear zone, stick to it. If you make an exception, you give the message that you really are interruptible, despite your plan.

Creative Procrastination: Allow yourself some time to procrastinate. Acknowledge that whatever you're doing instead is probably helpful. You might clean up your desk, do some creative art work, or take a walk. All of these have merit. When you let tasks bubble on the back burner, you can more easily see which tasks can fall away and which you really need to do.

Get Help: There are literally hundreds of thousands of advisors, practitioners, and assistants available to help you, many of whom just love doing what you hate doing. Get clear on what you need. Ask people you trust for referrals, bearing in mind that the person who's right for your friend may not be right for you. Talk to those who have used the person. Interview the helper before launching in. Evaluate the relationship and, if necessary, back out. Honor your own needs and get them fulfilled.

Replenish Resources: Write down activities that replenish your resources. Be sure to include entries in these areas—food, rest, stimulus, emotional contact, connection with nature, connection with Source, physical challenge. Fill your resource tank daily. Check to see which areas feel empty and start filling there. Enter the date and activity in your resource list. Review the list regularly to fill in the holes and add new activities.

Reset Button: Push the Reset Button to break up the behavior that's getting you into trouble. Pause, step out of the action, feeling, or thought, and step back in, but in a different way. Physical techniques can help. Widen your visual field to take in a broader scene; the difficult behavior may not be so compelling. Take a few slow breaths to center yourself inside your body and slow down. Take a walk, do some exercise, or just change your body position; moving can help other aspects of you move, too. Notice something interesting in the environment—an attractive color in a person's clothing, the light coming in a window, the movement of air. Remember that even in a situation that's uncomfortable, both "good" and "bad" coexist.

Space Invader Challenge: In this role play exercise, done with another person or in a small group, you identify difficult feelings that come up when somebody "invades your space." First, recall a scenario where somebody threw you off your agenda. Next, set up a role play in which you, the Invaded One, coach your partner in the role play to act the part of the Invader, the person who throws you off. Next, try a brief role play in which the Invader invades for a minute or two, acting just as that difficult person does. During the minute, you, as the Invaded One, don't respond in any way; you merely note the feelings that come up. Stop the role play, write down the feelings, and reflect on them. When you find yourself feeling angry and frustrated, or you push people away, it's evidence that your boundaries are too hard. When you feel overwhelmed, guilty, or confused, it's evidence that your boundaries are too soft. Think of what you might do to maintain a firm, yet flexible boundary—one that's not too hard or too soft.

Three-phase Close-Down: Contain the time you spend on a task by setting a timer and allowing one-quarter to one-third of the total time for close-down. While the timer is ticking you can work freely and intensely, knowing you'll have time to disengage. When the alarm rings, stop and move into the three-phase close-down. First, attend to the past—acknowledge the progress thus far. Next, attend to the future—write down the very next step so that when you come back, you can pick up right where you left off. Lastly, attend to the present—gather all the papers, put the next step trigger-note on top, and move the project to the side. Now you can disengage from the task, satisfied with a job well begun, confident that you know exactly where to begin again, and with a clear desk ready for whatever's next.

Time for Little Things: Dedicate some time to the little tasks that are easy to put off. As you go through the week put reminders about little things in a jar. That way you won't have to hold them in your head. Take fifteen minutes to a half hour once a week to draw from the jar and do them. Doing little things regularly washes down any static clinging to them and builds confidence that you will actually get to them.

Choice Practices

Closing Open Loops: Open loops are actions you have made a commitment to do but have not completed. By closing the loops, you reclaim their energy and make it available for other tasks. Closing the loop doesn't necessarily mean doing the action. In fact, deciding not to do it at all can close the loop. To close open loops, check to see if you have already completed the action, if it's irrelevant, or if it's impossible. If it's none of the above, decide whether you truly think it's worth doing. If so, finish it—this is often best—or decide when and how you are going to finish it. If you decide it's not worth finishing, make a clear decision that it's all right not to finish it *ever*. Then, do not worry about it anymore.

Crystal Time Management Tracker: This practice tracks where you put your energy in terms of the East Indian chakra system. You'll need a cup or small bowl placed on a saucer and a number of small crystals or stones in rainbow colors. Each chakra, or energy vortex along the spine, governs an area of life. For example, the first chakra has to do with survival issues like exercising the body and having good food. (See Further Reading for more information.) The chakras are associated with rainbow colors, from the lowest, red, to the highest, indigo. Use the crystal tracker to see how often you do the tasks of each chakra. At the beginning of the week, start with all the crystals in the cup. Whenever you put in time in the realm of the chakra, say, by having a 4th chakra heart interchange with a friend, take a crystal of the chakra color (in this instance, green) from the cup and move it to the saucer. Continue through the week. At the end of the week count up how many of each color are on the saucer. Most of us favor activities of some chakras while neglecting others. Use the tracker to balance your activities so one chakra doesn't overpower the others.

Decision Sieve: Here is a no-brainer way to reveal your preferences when faced with a decision.

Assign each possibility a number. Then compare each possibility one at a time to every other possibility using the grid below. Circle the possibility you prefer in each pair.

1	1	1	1	1	1	1	1
2	3	4	5	6	7	8	9
	2	2	2	2	2	2	2
	3	4	5	6	7	8	9
		3	3	3	3	3	3
		4	5	6	7	8	9
			4	4	4	4	4
			5	6	7	8	9
				5	5	5	5
				6	7	8	9
					6	6	6
					7	8	9
						7	7
						8	9
							8
							9

Count how many times you circled each number; enter the number for each below

1: ___ 2: ___ 3: ___ 4: ___ 5: ___ 6: ___ 7: ___ 8: ___ 9: ___

Arrange possibilities in order of the most "votes"

1st choice: _____ 4th choice: _____ 7th choice: _____

2nd choice: _____ 5th choice: _____ 8th choice: _____

3rd choice: _____ 6th choice: _____ 9th choice: _____

Divination: Experiment with divination methods to help you make choices. You ask a question and the method provides an answer. Such answers purportedly come from deeper knowledge than your mind's immediate reasons and justifications. Commonly used methods are I Ching, dowsing, various decks of cards, and runes (see the Further Reading for helpful books). Even what appears to be a wrong choice can yield unanticipated learning and benefits.

The Done List: At the end of the day, reflect on what you did, not to point a finger, but to learn from yourself and make things better. What choice factors were involved? Was what you chose to do attractive, important, beneficial, and/or urgent? What felt really good about what you did—what about doing it made you feel so good? What felt not-so-good—what about it felt bad? When you reflect, be sure to let satisfaction bloom. Everything is useful, even the things that don't happen as you would like.

Feeling Projection: At a choice point, imagine playing out each option into the future. Notice which option feels good and which feels bad. Take these feeling projections into account as you make your choice.

Letting Desire Show Up: Give desire an opportunity to present itself by taking an attraction walk. Go to Main Street or the mall and notice what draws your attention positively. Out of all the shop windows, which display pleases you the most; which colors on the rack of clothes attract you; which voices you overhear engage you? The more you pay attention to attraction and desire, the more it can help you make choices based on what feels good.

The MIT: Use this procedure to identify the most important task among the many important tasks on your list. Make six 3 x 5 cards with one important task on each. Lay them out so you can see all of them at once. Within this sample, identify one item that's more important than the others; put it on your right. Within what remains, identify the least important item; put that on your left. You have just defined a scale from Least Important to Most Important. Compare each remaining item to those at the poles, and arrange them along the scale. Most will fall somewhere in the middle. If there are more important tasks on your list, bring them into the scale, a few at a time. Now stack the items with the most important on top, the least important on the bottom. Work from top to bottom, knowing that you'll be giving more of your attention to the more important items. Generally, in any collection of items, 80% of the significance in the entire collection resides in only 20% of the items (the 80/20 Rule). The trick is to bring what's most significant to the foreground while letting the rest of the items fall into in the background.

Quality Levels: Instead of assuming that you must do everything perfectly, set a range of quality levels. The most common level is Business-As-Usual—perfectly adequate to the task, although not necessarily perfect. You could think of this as the 85–90% level on which you operate 85–90% of the time. Then there's the Bells-and-Whistles to hit when resources are abundant—plenty of time, money, and people power. When a new task comes in, also identify the Quick-And-Dirty—the bare minimum to do if you're going to do it at all. Even though you expect to be operating at Business-As-Usual, have the Quick-And-Dirty level in mind so that if the time frame shifts or resources are withdrawn you have a Plan B to fall back on.

Untangling Choice Factors: These factors are involved when making a choice: Important (how does this align with our/my mission), Urgent (how time sensitive is it), Attractive (how much do I want to do it), Beneficial (how much benefit does it give). When you have trouble choosing between tasks, put each task on a separate card. Then go through the cards and rate the factors on a scale of one to ten, with ten being high (very important, very urgent, very attractive, very beneficial). When all the score are six or above, you'll do it. When there's a wide disparity between the scores (for example, it's ten on Important and one on Attractive), use the three-phase close-down to contain the time you spend with it. At least you will have done something on it. If you tend to do whatever is quick and easy, you'll spend time on trivia and neglect what's important. The three-phase close-down equalizes the Quick factor by allowing you to use short snippets of time regardless of how long the entire task takes. "Sticky" project management equalizes the Easy factor by breaking the task down so that all components are equally doable.

What Do I Have to Give Up to Get What I Want?: Do this brainstorm with a current troublesome issue that you would like to change. First, imagine the issue completely resolved; it's no longer an issue. Really put yourself there. Then, brainstorm what about your current behavior would you have to give up in order to resolve the issue. What would you have to say "No" to in order to say "Yes" to the change that will resolve the issue. When you take these steps, you identify what's holding you back from making the change. In order to open the way to change, you'll need to make peace with whatever is holding you back and let it go.

Work & Play, Body & Soul, Cycles & Surprises: Group items on your To Do list into six categories. *Work* activities contribute to your engaged presence in the world, like a job (paid or not). *Play* activities offer simple enjoyment or opportunities to experiment with life, like watching a movie or reading a novel. *Body* activities promote physical flexibility, strength, coordination, and body awareness, like working out or going for a walk. *Soul* activities promote self-awareness, personal growth, and interrelationship, like journaling, attending church services, or dream interpretation. *Cycles* activities recur on a regular basis, like doing laundry, buying a car, or brushing your teeth. *Surprises* activities are, by definition, unexpected. Do task sessions in each category every day. Mix them up so you don't follow one session with another of the same category, in fact, don't repeat a category until you've put in time with each of the others.

FEELING-HABITS

Over the twenty-plus years I've been teaching and consulting I've heard from hundreds, perhaps thousands, of individual clients and group participants about their feeling-habits. Here is a sample, written in the first person, listed alphabetically, with ideas on how to work with them. You'll notice that feeling-habits that seem very different to you are grouped together. That's because they may have similar underlying patterns and potential remedies.

There are no hard and fast rules about feeling-habits; your experience may be very different. Take what you can from these characterizations and follow your feeling-habits back to the leverage point where you can apply some effort. They're worth tracking down.

Addicted to Productivity (also fear of failure): I have to be productive all the time. If I'm not, it's a waste, and that's intolerable. As soon as I'm done with one project I'm on to the next. I continually prove myself to others and top my best achievements. I'm an essential, valuable member of society because of my productivity. I track these feelings back to a deep insecurity about my self-worth. At this leverage point, I look squarely in the mirror with unconditional, compassionate acceptance, whether I'm productive or not, and find true security and self-worth there.

Afraid of Success: I'm worried that if I do something really successful I'll get more work. People will expect me to answer all their questions. They won't treat me as a fellow human being. I won't be able to hide in the background anymore. I'll have to maintain a standard that will be just too high to keep up. The successful people I've known are arrogant and self-important. I track these feelings back to an unwillingness to own my power and a fear of becoming de-humanized. At this leverage point, I acknowledge that I do have influence. I take care to exercise my power well. I put realistic limits on what I do. And I stay in touch with my humanity and humility.

Angry (also rebellious, irritated, frustrated, impatient, arrogant, blaming, "if only" conditionality): I get angry when I feel that everybody else is messing up. If only they would stop doing what they're doing, everything would be just fine. I track this feeling-habit (and its fellows) back to my need to place responsibility outside myself. From there I feel that if I do accept responsibility, I'm going to have to change the world and that's just too overwhelming. At this leverage point, I step onto the bank of the river of experience and see my own contribution to the situation as well as everyone else's. Then, I do what I can, contained within good task boundaries.

Distracted (also restless, scattered, over-absorbed, worried, regretful): I'm easily distracted. Everything takes me away from what I have to do. I can't quite settle down and get into it. Yet if I do, I become so deeply absorbed I can't come up for air. I worry a lot about what might happen. I also have a lot of regret about the past. Tracking this feeling-habit back, I see how uncomfortable I am with what's happening now and with my emotions as they arise. At this leverage point, I breathe and stay present. I cultivate centered attention within an appropriate boundary. I acknowledge that even difficult emotions come with valuable lessons, so I welcome them as teachers. In so doing, I accept my entire experience.

Embarrassed (also ashamed, guilty, self-deprecating, wanting to do what everyone else is doing, wanting to do the right thing, afraid of making the wrong choice): I get embarrassed when I make a mistake and look foolish. I know I'm smarter than that, but I goofed, and there it is. I track this feeling-habit back to looking outside myself for validation. From there I track the need for outside validation to not feeling legitimate, not feeling that I have a right to be here, to take up space, to breathe the air. At this leverage point, I practice satisfaction. I acknowledge what I do, from the inside, not the outside. I set a firm, yet flexible boundary to protect my vulnerable self, and keep building up evidence that I do have a right to be here. After all, I *am* here!

Fatigued (also *discouraged, despairing, resigned, overwhelmed, helpless, depleted, stuffed, wistful, longing, paralyzed):* I get tired just thinking of everything I have to do. I track this feeling-habit back to a place where I see I've taken on a lot of fuzzy, generalized expectations, which, because they're so unclear, are impossible to fulfill. The fatigue shuts me down so I don't do anything, or I drag myself through whatever I do manage to accomplish. At this leverage point, I set my boundaries well, cultivate satisfaction, and most importantly, say "No." I rekindle desire and rediscover what draws me on. And I'm gentle with myself.

Wanting It Solved Once-and-For-All (also *wanting it already done, stuck in the future or the past):* I wish everything could just be fixed so I can "get on with it" (whatever "it" is). I track this feeling-habit back to discomfort with not only how things are right now, but also with the fact that things are in continual flux. Behind these feelings is an unwillingness to commit to being here on earth. At that leverage point, I center my attention within myself. I get my internal allies to support me. I make the choice to Be Here Now and play the game according to Planet Earth rules, where things do change.

Wanting It to Be Perfect: I can't let something just be—it has to be perfect. Tracking this feeling-habit back, I see that I think I already know what the result should be. I measure myself against a self-imposed standard. At this leverage point, I try, instead, to open myself to new information and feel my way through by attending to my heart and intuition as much as to a pre-set standard.

Wanting to Put It Off (procrastination): I keep putting things off mainly because if I finish, then I'll know the outcome, and it certainly won't be good! Procrastination is embarrassment in advance along with a bit of you-can't-make-me rebelliousness. Tracking this feeling-habit back, I find that trust and acceptance make all the difference. I accept the result, whatever it is. I trust that what I do will be perfectly sufficient. Satisfaction practice at every juncture helps, too.

Feeling-habits act like smokescreens or buffers between ourselves and the real issues. We attend to The Lesser at the expense of The Greater. If we actually resolve the real issue, then we'll have to change. If we change, then we'll have no excuses—we'll have to buckle down and get on with it. Keep in mind that the whole point of time management isn't to buckle down and get through the To Do list. It's to live our lives to the fullest. (Those two things, by the way, need not be mutually exclusive.)

TO CONTACT PAM KRISTAN

For an *Awakening in Time* retreat, seminar, talk or consultation see Pam's Website www.pamelakristan.com or e-mail her at pam@pamelakristan.com.

LaVergne, TN USA
16 June 2010
186264LV00001B/4/P